the 7 Principles of an Evangelistic Life

the 7 PRINCIPLES of an EVANGELISTIC Life

Douglas M. Cecil

MOODY PUBLISHERS
CHICAGO

All Scripture quotations, unless otherwise indicated, are taken from the *New American Standard Bible*®, Copyright © The Lockman Foundation 1960, 1962, 1963, 1968, 1971, 1972, 1973, 1975, 1977, 1995. Used by permission.

Scripture quotations marked NIV are taken from the *Holy Bible, New International Version*®. NIV®. Copyright © 1973, 1978, 1984 by International Bible Society. Used by permission of Zondervan Publishing House. All rights reserved.

Library of Congress Cataloging-in-Publication Data

Cecil, Douglas M., 1952-
    The seven principles of an evangelistic life / Douglas M. Cecil.
        p. cm.
    Includes bibliographical references.
    ISBN 0-8024-0924-5
    1. Evangelistic work. 2. Christian life. I. Title.

BV3793.C43 2003
269'.2--dc21

2003005465

1 3 5 7 9 10 8 6 4 2

Printed in the United States of America

to my bride of thirty years,

Patty,

who has continued to encourage me

to abide in Christ

CONTENTS

PART 2: PRACTICAL PROCLAMATION

FOREWORD

—

THE WORD "EVANGELISTIC" has faded and frayed in the storm of religious fervor and propaganda sweeping through the world's jittery population. Haunted by guerilla tactics on nearly every continent, thinking people cower at the thought of being approached by someone with strong convictions.

Evangelism is defined generically in the American Heritage Dictionary as "the zealous preaching and dissemination of the Gospel, as through missionary work." Thanks to our modern secular media, preachers and missionaries are often identified with oddballs—either pale, beady-eyed creatures intent on casting some sort of spell on others, or a hyped-up quasi-entertainer with a hard-sell approach to a particular brand of belief.

The "evangel" is the good news about what God has done for the hopeless plight of mankind. No one should be denied the privilege of hearing about events that are critically important to life and death. Yet the Enemy tries constantly to obscure the facts with his own "spin" to paint a veneer of ridicule and contempt over the truth.

Nowhere does God command unbelievers to go to church, but the Bible clearly commands believers to penetrate the world with His message. Some are particularly gifted at addressing large numbers of people with the Good News, and God moves on the hearts of the hearers to respond in faith. Others are incredibly effective with small groups or in private encounters, presenting the simple truth that God loves the world and receives anyone who will turn and believe in Him.

Christian lifestyle remains in the minds of most believers as an optional choice. Our human propensity for doing what we please, currently termed our "rights," seems to justify that we can live in our culture according to our desires and simply add on whatever church affiliation makes us feel most comfortable. On a hospital entrance form we would check the space for "Christian" to designate what form of burial we might require.

Many of us forget that following Christ requires resignation of our rights, that we have signed on to please Him, not ourselves. This is a key theme in Doug Cecil's book *The 7 Principles of an Evangelistic Life.* Christ's will is that all will come to believe Him, and that requires unremitting vigilance for every believer. Every contact with us should be like hopping into a demo automobile to enjoy the luxury of a few minutes with a real God-like person.

This book pulls into clear focus how a believer should behave on a daily basis. Since God leaves us here in this world after we place our faith in His Son, instead of taking us immediately home to heaven, His purpose is that we are to become spiritual lighthouses and a purifying element in a decaying society—no matter our specific occupations.

With our hereditary baggage of sin and our cultural peer pressure distorting the very idea of a loving God, the task of living every day as a reflection of His grace becomes a challenge. Doug Cecil has translated abstract daily life into practical how-tos, the art of living an example for others to see the power of the Christ-life everyday.

HOWARD G. HENDRICKS
Distinguished Professor and Chairman
Center for Christian Leadership
Dallas Theological Seminary

ACKNOWLEDGMENTS

A BOOK GOES through many stages. I am deeply grateful to many who played a part in making this book possible.

I am thankful to the faculty, staff, and administration of Dallas Theological Seminary who have allowed me the opportunity to grow and develop. The faculty have always challenged me with their commitment to biblical excellence and accuracy. The staff have always encouraged me with their sacrificial service. The administration have always inspired me with their vision, faithfulness, and commitment to "staying the course."

I thank the long line of Bible teachers, mentors, and colleagues who have influenced and changed my thinking over the years. Anyone in the Christian life knows that most of the ideas probably came from someone else and are just distilled and compiled here for your reading. Thank you to those faithful servants who have gone before.

I thank the students of Dallas Seminary who over the years have challenged my thinking and have helped crystallize my thoughts. Many of their thoughts have become my thoughts.

A special thanks to Mrs. Shannon Stevens who read the manuscript to make sure that each sentence had a verb. I also extend warm thanks to my close friend Reverend Jeff Townsend. Jeff is a gifted Bible teacher with a keen mind for detail. All of his suggestions were incorporated into the final draft. He sacrificially gave of himself to minister to me in this way.

I thank Moody Publishers for having the courage to print a book on evangelism. That is not normal for publishing houses today. Moody has a history of being on the front lines of evangelicalism and challenging the church and believers to a radical dependence upon Jesus Christ.

INTRODUCTION

EVANGELISM. The word stirs our deepest emotions. Some—believers and unbelievers—cringe and shiver at the word. Others squirm at the thought. Many try to ignore the concept altogether. And still others get excited upon hearing the word.

Evangelism is one of those topics that everybody (Christian and unbeliever) has an opinion about. And usually everybody is emotionally attached to whatever opinion he or she holds. So why another book on the topic?

The goal of this book is to bring a sense of balance back to evangelism. Evangelism seems to have drifted into individual personal "styles." A believer is challenged to find his or her personal "style" of evangelism; your "style" is whatever you choose as your own preference. If you feel comfortable with your personal "style," then that is all that matters.

However, there are still people who are lost and couldn't care less about your own personal style of evangelism! Evangelism is not about you. Evangelism is about God and what He has done through Jesus

Christ. This book seeks to bring some balance back into our approach to reaching people for Jesus Christ.

A believer needs to be authentic and real in sharing the Good News. That authenticity comes only through the Holy Spirit. It is a spiritual thing. We need to rely totally upon the Holy Spirit and love people the way God loves people. We need to see people the way God sees people. You can't manufacture love for people in the flesh. You can't conjure up evangelism. It is the Holy Spirit who works through believers to take the message of salvation to an unbelieving world. We are just tools that God chooses to use to communicate His message.

You can have the slickest methods going, yet if the Holy Spirit is not in it, nothing is going to happen. Only God is able to lift that veil that blinds men's eyes toward the Gospel. Only God is able to bring about conversion.

So this is not another book on evangelism methods. Methods come and go. Often evangelism is seen as only the work and responsibility of the believer. The truth defended in these pages is relying upon the Holy Spirit for the work of evangelism.

What is recorded here has been gleaned during the past thirty years of my own Christian adventure. I am not perfect. This work is not exhaustive. I am a normal guy with a burden. I plod along in the spiritual life trying to be faithful to what God has called me to do. This book is merely a signpost in the journey.

Developing an evangelistic lifestyle begins with your relationship with Jesus Christ. Evangelism flows from your personal relationship with the living Savior. Evangelism is a spiritual adventure. It is from that perspective that I humbly offer these thoughts.

PART ONE:
PERSONAL PREPARATION

ONE:
FLY THE AIRPLANE!

EVANGELISM PRINCIPLE 1: *Keep your priorities straight.*

I STARTED FLYING AIRPLANES about the same time that I started driving cars. In fact, I had the privilege of earning my private pilot's license when I was eighteen years old. My father, a veteran pilot with thousands of hours of flying time, taught me how to fly.

My father was also a very disciplined pilot, so there were a few extra "procedures" that went along with me learning to fly. I probably had the most extensive preflight checklist that had ever been designed. We checked everything! It seemed to me that my checklist was a book.

But I will always remember that my father had only one checklist item when it came to the "emergency checklist." That one checklist item was "Fly the airplane." It was a very simple, straightforward, and basic statement.

You see, when an emergency happens in the cockpit, it is easy for the pilot to get distracted. A lot of airplane accidents happen when a distracted pilot flies a perfectly good airplane into the ground because his attention is momentarily drawn somewhere else. Hence, the first emergency checklist item reminds you of the very basics. First, make sure that you fly the airplane. Go back to the basics. Once you have the airplane under control, then you work the problem.

When you come to the subject of evangelism, it is difficult to know where to start. After all, there are so many different strategies that are out there. When is it appropriate to employ a relational strategy? When is it appropriate to be more aggressive? Should we argue evidences for the faith? The various approaches to evangelism can be like the distractions in the cockpit.

THE IMPORTANCE OF YOUR PRIORITIES

So where do you begin to sort all of this out? You go back to the basics. You go back to the one main item on the checklist. You begin by talking about why you are doing what you are doing. For evangelism to be effective, you have to keep your priorities in order. So for us to begin our study, let me talk about priorities.

Priorities are important. Priorities help guide decisions that we make about the use of our time and our money. They are like a lighthouse in the midst of a storm or a landmark to focus upon in the forest when things get rough. Where can we go to find those priorities? I think our Lord understood our need for priorities when He comforted His disciples in the Upper Room prior to His arrest.

John 13–16 records the Upper Room Discourse, Jesus' last in-depth communication with His disciples before going to the cross. The following chapter, John 17, records His High Priestly Prayer, which is Jesus' prayer for His disciples in light of His impending departure from this world.

In the Upper Room Discourse, Jesus is about to leave His disciples. It is the evening of the Last Supper, and it is the night in which Jesus will be betrayed. In an upstairs room in Jerusalem, gathered for the Passover Feast, the twelve disciples listen as Jesus begins to lay out three priorities for them. He will summarize everything that He has said over the past three years.

John 13 records Jesus demonstrating what it means to truly have love for one another (John 13:35) by washing His disciples' feet. His comments, however, to Judas Iscariot in John 13:21–30 troubled His disciples.

In response, Jesus deals with the disciples' troubled hearts. He talks about a place in heaven that has been prepared for them (John 14:1–14). He tells them about the Holy Spirit who will come to them as a Helper and Guide (John 14:15–26). He talks about peace (John 14:27–31). Jesus says in John 14:27, "Peace I leave with you; My peace I give to you; not as the world gives do I give to you. Let not your heart be troubled, nor let it be fearful."

Then in John 15, Jesus begins to instruct His disciples. He leaves directions for His disciples for when He will no longer be with them. As Jesus begins to address His disciples in this chapter, He is, in essence, saying, "I am about to leave you, and there are three priorities that you need to hear. There are a couple of items that I think are important. There are a few priorities in life that will help to guide you after I leave." Jesus then outlines three priorities in life that His disciples should follow.[1]

In John 16, Jesus once again speaks about the ministry of the Holy Spirit. He talks about how the Holy Spirit will glorify Him. He speaks about His return and how they might have peace and courage.

And then, amazingly, in the High Priestly Prayer recorded in John 17, Jesus prays for the same three priorities that He just gave in the Upper Room Discourse in John 15. If these priorities are what Jesus Christ desired to communicate to His disciples before He left, we need to pay attention to what He is saying. What are these three priorities?

PRIORITY 1: ABIDE IN JESUS

The first thing that He says in John 15:4–5 is *abide in Christ.* "Abide in Me, and I in you," Jesus commands. "As the branch cannot bear fruit of itself unless it abides in the vine, so neither can you unless you abide in Me. I am the vine, you are the branches; he who abides in Me and I in him, he bears much fruit, for apart from Me you can do nothing."

The word *abide* means to remain, stay, or continue. In other words, the disciples are to remain, or continue, in their relationship with Christ. We have been created to be dependent upon Christ. Abiding in Jesus means to believe in Him and continue to follow Him. Jesus may have had Judas in mind as one who did not abide in Christ. Judas failed to continue to follow Him. Judas appeared to be a follower and a disciple, but was not.

The Father is the vinedresser (15:1) and is interested in fruitfulness. Jesus is the true vine (15:1), and we are the branches (15:5). In essence, fruitful people are Christlike people.

Fruit is the manifestation of Christian character in a broad sense. Bearing fruit is living according to Scripture, which stands in contrast to an unbeliever who refuses to submit to Christ's biblical teaching. Bearing fruit would include evangelism and other qualities that would give evidence of one's faith in Christ.

The passage does not read, "Apart from Me you can do some things," or, "Apart from Me you can be effective in ministry," or, "Apart from Me you can have an effective outreach in evangelism." No, what the Bible says is, "Apart from Me you can do nothing."

Granted, you are going to be able to do some things (nonbelievers do things all the time), but what you are about to do under your own power will amount to nothing but wood, hay, and stubble. Your works in the flesh will be of the flesh. All of the works that you do in the flesh will be burned up (1 Corinthians 3:11–15).

Above everything else in life, we are to be committed first to Jesus Christ. Our relationship with Jesus Christ needs to be first in our life, our top priority. First above anything else is Jesus Christ.

That first priority is emphasized throughout the Scriptures, from God's words to Israel after the Exodus, "Hear, O Israel, the Lord your God is one. Love the Lord with all your heart, with all your soul, with all your strength" (Deuteronomy 6:4 paraphrased), to the New Testament admonition to "fix your thoughts on Jesus" and later to "fix your eyes on Jesus" (Hebrews 3:1 NIV; 12:2). The book of Revelation, the Bible's finale, focuses on Christ and concludes with the worship of God.

Recall Jesus' answer to a Pharisee lawyer:

"Teacher, which is the great commandment in the Law?" And [Jesus] said to him, "'You shall love the Lord your God will all your heart, and with all your soul, and with all your mind.' This is the great and foremost commandment." (Matthew 22:36–38)

The Scriptures continue to cry out that our first priority needs to be Jesus Christ. Apart from Him we can do nothing. Every aspect of our life needs to be lived with that priority clearly cemented in our brain.

> The greatest obstacle to [evangelism] is the church
> that is preoccupied with its own existence.

If the church is centered on anything—on anyone, on any doctrine, on any project—apart from Jesus Christ, it is off balance. Beware of those things that might try to drag us away from that first freshness of knowing Jesus Christ. Beware of those kicks, of those fads, of those silly gimmicks that twenty years from now will be passé and discarded because they did not work.

I believe that the greatest obstacle to the evangelization of the world is the church that is preoccupied with its own existence rather than focused upon Jesus Christ. We must be willing to put all of our activities and all of our efforts on trial before the judgment seat of Jesus Christ.

Having Jesus Christ first in our church begins with Jesus Christ being first with us individually. Jesus Christ first in our church begins with our individual worship. Is Jesus Christ first in your life? It begins with our personal devotional life. With Christ as the center of our lives there is movement, there is arrangement, there is direction, and there is empowerment.

Christ becomes the center of our lives only when abiding in Him is foremost in our thoughts. Your wife or your husband cannot be first. He or she is a companion along the way. Your children cannot be first. Scholarship cannot be first. Personal ministry, no matter how vital or successful, cannot be first. Your church cannot be first or you will burn out. You yourself cannot be first. Jesus Christ needs to be first in your life. Apart from Him nothing is going to happen.

How do you know when God is first in your life? The fruit of the Spirit will be manifested. You will experience love, joy, peace, patience, kindness, goodness, faithfulness, gentleness, and self-control (Galatians 5:22–23).

Where you spend your time and your money is going to be a good indication of your first priority in life. When I started dating my wife more than thirty years ago, how did Patty know that she was the focus of my attention? How did she know that she was my priority? She could tell because of my focus in life. What is first in your life?

PRIORITY 2: LOVE ONE ANOTHER

The second priority that we see in chapter 15 is to *love one another.* Notice John 15:12, "This is My commandment, that you love one another, just as I have loved you." After Jesus told the Pharisee that the greatest commandment was to "love the Lord your God with all your heart, and with all your soul, and with all your mind," He noted a second great commandment. "The second is like it, 'You shall love your neighbor as yourself.' On these two commandments depend the whole Law and the Prophets" (Matthew 22:37–40).

We are first to abide in Christ, and then we are to love one another. That means we are to build one another up in love.

Once again, Scripture reaffirms that priority. Leviticus 19:18 reads, "Love your neighbor as yourself," and Deuteronomy 15:11 adds, "You shall freely open your hand to your brother."

"Love one another" is the most basic one-another command in the New Testament; however, there are many practical examples in the New Testament of what it means to love one another in the body of Christ. You read in Romans to "love one another,"[2] as well as to "be of the same mind toward one another," "[build] up . . . one another," and "admonish one another."[3] Other ways we are to love one another, according to the Scriptures, are to "care for one another," "serve one another," "bear one another's burdens," "be kind to one another," [and to] "be subject to one another."[4] The apostle James also tells us to "confess your sins to one another, and pray for one another" (5:16). We could go on and on and on with all the "one another" passages in the New Testament. There are many, many truths in Scripture that continue to point to the relationship we need to have with one another in Jesus Christ.

Notice in the John 15 passage that the type of love that we are to have for one another is a sacrificial love (v. 13). It is also an intimate love (vv. 14–15). Jesus no longer refers to His disciples as slaves but friends. But the love that we have for one another is also a fruitful love (vv. 16–17). The nature of our relationships with other Christian brothers and sisters should stimulate us toward greater fruitfulness. Are you the type of friend who stimulates a closer walk with the Savior, or are you more of a consumer in the relationship? Do you value your relationships within the body of Christ the same way that Jesus would value those relationships?

Paul said in 2 Corinthians 8:5, "And they did not do as we expected, but they gave themselves first to the Lord and then to us in keeping with God's will" (NIV). Priority number one is abide in Christ. Give yourself to the Lord. Priority number two is love one another. Give yourself to the brothers and sisters in Christ.

Loving one another begins with our own personal activity of worship and continues in the way that we reach out to people around us in the body of Jesus Christ. Reaching out, caring, and bearing one another's burdens within a local small group context is one way loving one another is going to spill out to a lost world.

Once we lead somebody to Jesus Christ, where is the first place we are going to take him or her? We are going to take that person to the local church. It is my prayer that the church reflects Christlike love.

PRIORITY 3: REACH THE WORLD

Third, we are not only to abide in Christ and love one another, but we are also to reach the world. Scripture says that you will bear witness. In John 15:16 we read that we are appointed to "go and bear fruit." When Jesus says "go," He is encouraging His disciples to look beyond the regular circle of His followers, reaching others with the love of Christ.

"Fruit" here refers not only to the fruit of the Spirit but also to a broad range of being fruitful for Christ. As we bear fruit, many will be touched for Jesus Christ.

Verses 26 and 27 of that chapter say, "He will testify about Me, and you will testify also." Because of the abiding presence of the Holy Spirit in our lives, we will be witnesses for Christ.

We do not have to go through the entire Bible to be able to accurately document priority number three. We read in the Old Testament in Psalm 67:2, "That Your way may be known on the earth, Your salvation among all nations." God said, "I will also make You a light of the nations so that My salvation may reach to the end of the earth" (Isaiah 49:6).

The New Testament makes it clear that the church is to take the Gospel to the world. It is extremely important for the health of the church that leaders continue to make courageous plans for evangelism. In fact, the whole book of Acts is the fulfillment of this call. In the book of Acts we see the message of Christ geographically and theologically taken by the power of the Holy Spirit from Jerusalem (the Jews) to Rome (the Gentiles).

Out of our commitment to Jesus Christ must flow our commitment to His church and to His body. When we are rich in His Word and experience the dynamic that we have with our Lord, then we can encourage God's people. When we are encouraged by His people, and we are fed and nourished by God's servants, then we will be committed to reach the world.

Evangelism is a natural expression of . . .
our relationship with Jesus Christ.

We see a commitment to the world demonstrated in the life of Jesus Christ. He was with the hungry. He was with the sick. He mingled with the crowd. He was with the street women. He was with the rich. He was with the woman who was divorced five times. All the way through Scripture we see Jesus continuing to reach out to the people around Him. There was no exclusivism. There was no sense of becoming ingrown in fellowship. The New Testament church was continually reaching out. It was continually spilling out and overflowing into the world.

When a relationship with and a commitment to Jesus Christ and His body, the church, is clearly evident, people can not help but be drawn to Him. They can not help but be drawn to the grace and mercy that is found in Him. In fact, they will climb trees to see Him, they will go without food to listen to Him, and they will tear the roof off of a house to get near Him.

Evangelism is a natural expression of everything else that's happening in our relationship with Jesus Christ. It's also a natural expression of everything that is happening to us in the body of Jesus Christ. As the world sees that visible incarnation of the body of Christ, it can not help but be drawn to the truth.

The entire fifteenth chapter of John talks about these three priorities: "abiding in Christ" (vv. 1–11), "loving one another" (vv. 12–17), and "reaching the world" (vv. 18–27). All the way through the chapter we see that the ultimate result is commitment to reaching the world for Jesus Christ.

HOW THE PRIORITIES RELATE

In John 17, the High Priestly Prayer, we see once again those three priorities. Here Jesus relates the three priorities to each other to give specific direction to ministry.

Notice in John 17:11, Jesus prays for the disciples, "Holy Father, keep them in Your name." This is a reference to priority number one, their relationship to God. Believers are to be kept in His name in order that "they may be one," which is a reference to priority number two, our relationship to others. Notice also the dependence of priority two on priority one. In other words, a healthy ministry within the body depends on believers having a wholesome walk with Jesus Christ.

But that is not all. In verse 21, Jesus takes things a step further, praying "that they may all be one." This is a reference to priority number two, "so that the *world* may believe that You sent me" (italics added), which is a reference to priority number three. Not only does Jesus teach His disciples these three priorities in the Upper Room Discourse, but then He prays for those same things in the High Priestly Prayer in John 17!

Growing in Christlikeness and helping others grow in Him are not the ends in themselves. Our Lord's desire is that these two priorities will, in turn, lead to winning a lost world to Jesus Christ. There is an outward flow that starts in our relationship with Jesus Christ. Abiding in Christ and loving one another leads to reaching the world for Him.

KEEPING A BALANCE

These three priorities must be kept in focus if there is to be balance in evangelism. Here is the main point: *There is a great commandment before there is a great commission.* You may have the slickest method, the slickest presentation, and be the most silver-tongued person around; but if your relationship with Jesus Christ is out of focus, evangelism is out of balance. Everything that happens in evangelism is a by-product of our personal relationship with Jesus Christ.

Remember, *out of our personal relationship with Jesus Christ flows our relationship with others and our relationship with the world.*

In Mark 1:17 Jesus says, "Follow Me, and I will make you become fishers of men." Priority number one flows into priority number three. If you are a follower, then you will be a fisher. A follower is a fisher. If you have priority number one straight, He will make you a fisher of men. If I put my name in this verse, it would read, "Doug, I want you to follow Me. And as you follow Me I will make you a fisher of men."

Evangelism is not our first priority. Our relationship with Jesus Christ is our first priority. However, evangelism is ultimately where the flow of Jesus' argument is headed in the Upper Room Discourse.

Balance is very important in the spiritual life. We must keep things in the proper perspective. We must continue to keep our priorities straight.

Likewise, we cannot just take one priority and focus on that alone. All three priorities should happen together. You cannot just take one and say, "Well, when I get this one all figured out, then I'll move to number two." If you do, you will be out of balance.

Christians need stimulation of personal relationships to help encourage love and good deeds. If we do not move out into the world, we will not have that stimulation that throws us back to Jesus Christ. All three priorities need to be a fundamental part of our lives all the time.

If you are focused on the wrong things, evangelism will be hindered. If you have your priorities straight with Jesus Christ, you are going to experience the fruit of the Spirit and the fruit overflowing into the world.

Where is your focus right now? Is Jesus Christ first in your life? Keep your priorities straight. Evangelism is a by-product of our relationship with Christ. Put Him first.

TWO:
YOU MAKE THE CALL!

SOME YEARS AGO an intriguing television commercial gave viewers the chance to make a referee's call on a particularly difficult football play. Viewers would see a film clip of one key play and then the announcer said, "You make the call." Then there was the pitch for the product, followed by the referee's decision. I don't remember what product they were selling, but I do remember some of the plays.

In that same spirit, "you make the call" on whether evangelism has taken place in the following scenarios:

- I mow my neighbor's yard. He knows that I am a "Christian"; however, I never have an opportunity to talk about spiritual things. You make the call. Did I do evangelism?
- I volunteer at a local hospital as a hospital chaplain. I wear a hospital badge that clearly identifies me as a chaplain, and my presence is known and appreciated in the hospital. You make the call. Is my Christian presence in the hospital doing evangelism?
- I invite a couple to church. They attend the service, we have a

nice lunch together, and then we go to our homes. You make the call. Did I do evangelism?

- Your church has a food pantry. Your church distributes food to needy families in the community all under the banner of Christianity. You make the call. Is your church doing evangelism?
- I am sitting on an airplane next to an atheist. During the discussion about spiritual matters God is able to use me to move that person's position from being an atheist to an agnostic. You make the call. Did I do evangelism?

DEFINITION, PLEASE

The answer to all of the above scenarios depends upon how you choose to define evangelism. What is evangelism? When you think of evangelism, what comes to your mind? Is evangelism merely letting your light shine wherever you may be?

Maybe when you think of evangelism you think about a professional evangelist. Perhaps you think of a local church visitation program. Or do you think that evangelism is just an aggressive mission to confront people with the Gospel?

What is evangelism? And when does evangelism take place? When is the believer doing the work of an evangelist (2 Timothy 4:5)? Would you say that evangelism is more of an *event,* or would you say that evangelism is more of a *process* that takes place over a long period of time?

Trying to define evangelism can at times be very confusing. Everybody seems to have a different definition of evangelism and a different understanding of when we are engaged in doing the work of an evangelist. Even noted authors on evangelism differ on the definition. Some define evangelism as an event, whereas others take the position that evangelism is more of a process. Some see evangelism in a personal sense, and others see evangelism in a social sense. Are we to change the individual to impact the world, or are we to change the world to impact the individual? What does the Bible say?

In this chapter we will discuss the definition of evangelism. In a future chapter we will discuss the definition of the Gospel. The definition of evangelism centers around two main ideas.

COMMUNICATING THE GOOD NEWS OF JESUS CHRIST

Scripture centers the definition of evangelism on proclaiming the good news of Jesus Christ. You will not find the word *evangelism* in Scripture. However, you will find the word *evangelist* three times in Scripture, which is as close as you are going to get. *Evangelism* is an English word derived from the Greek language in which the New Testament was originally penned. We tend to use the word as a noun. To better understand where we get the word *evangelism,* it is helpful to become familiar with three Greek words. There are only three words that apply. We will look at them in succession, as the argument tends to build off the previous word.[1]

The first Greek word that is helpful to understand is the word *euangelion.* In 1 Corinthians 15:1–2 we read: "Now I make known to you, brethren, the gospel [the Good News] which I preached to you, which also you received, in which also you stand, by which also you are saved, if you hold fast the word which I preached to you, unless you believed in vain."

Notice in this verse that Paul stressed that this is the Gospel—the good news that the Corinthians received, stand in, and are saved by. In fact, in verse 11 Paul stated that this was the Gospel that they believed.

In verses 3 through 5 Paul explained what is included in that Good News. The word that's used in verse 1 for "gospel" is the Greek word *euangelion,* which means "good news." It is used here as a noun. What is that Good News? Paul explained that the Good News (the *euangelion*) is that Christ died for our sins and arose from the dead. The Good News is Christ's substitutionary atonement and resurrection.

The second Greek word that is helpful to understand is the word *euangelizo.* In 1 Corinthians 1:17 we read, "For Christ did not send me to baptize, but to preach the gospel." "Preach the gospel" is the English translation of the one Greek word *euangelizo.* The word *euangelizo,* the verb form of *euangelion,* means "to announce or to proclaim the Good News." What is the Good News? To find the definition of what we are to preach we go back to 1 Corinthians 15:3–5: the Good News (*euangelion*) is that Christ died for our sins and arose from the dead.

> Evangelism centers on proclaiming that
> Christ died for our sins and arose from the dead.

The third Greek word that is helpful to understand is the word *euangelistes.* This word appears only three times in Scripture and builds off of the previous two words. In Ephesians 4:11 we read, "And He gave some as . . . evangelists." The word that is translated "evangelists" is *euangelistes* and means "one who announces or proclaims the Good News." The word comes from the verb and is used as a noun. We see the word again in 2 Timothy 4:5 when we are called to "do the work of an evangelist." The last place that we find the word is describing Philip in Acts 21:8, "Philip the evangelist." Philip is one who announces or proclaims the Good News. Paul has already told us what the Good News (*euangelion*) is in 1 Corinthians 15:3–5: Christ died for our sins and arose from the dead.

The point is that whatever the word *evangelism* means, it appears that doing the work of an evangelist (*euangelistes*), or doing evangelism, centers on the proclamation of the Good News (*euangelion*). Doing evangelism centers on proclaiming that Christ died for our sins and arose from the dead.

INTENDING TO INVITE
THE LISTENER TO TRUST CHRIST

Other passages seem to add other definitions, or other elements, that might be included in our definition. In Acts 14:15 Barnabas and Paul told the people of Lystra, "[We] preach the gospel to you [in order] that you should turn from these vain things to a living God." Not only are we to preach the Gospel, which seems to be focused around the good news of Jesus Christ, but we are to preach the Gospel with the *intent* that something should happen.

In Matthew 4:19 Jesus challenges His disciples with the words, "Follow Me, and I will make you fishers of men." Let's think for a minute about the figure of speech that Jesus uses of being "fishers of men." We get up early in the morning, grab our rod, reel, hook, and our worm, and wander out to the local pond. When we arrive at the shore, we take our rod and throw the line with our hook and worm out into the water. What is the intent as we engage in the activity of fishing? Is the intent to drown that poor worm? Is the intent to sit on the shore of the pond and watch the ripples? Of course not. The intent is to catch fish.

The intent that Jesus had for His disciples when He said, "I will make you fishers of men" is that we would go forth and catch people. Jesus was in essence saying, "There is an intent that goes with following Me. The intent is that I will make you fishers of men."

There is an intent that goes with the proclamation of the Gospel. We preach the Gospel in order that something might take place. Information without intention is merely instruction. *Evangelism always preaches the Gospel with the intent that something would happen.*

ELEMENTS *NOT* TO BE INCLUDED
IN OUR DEFINITION OF EVANGELISM

Are there any other elements that should be included in our definition? Remember that right now we are just looking at the definition of evangelism. Later we will discuss elements that some suggest should be included in the Gospel message.

Doesn't Colossians 1:28—"We proclaim Him, admonishing every man and teaching every man with all wisdom, so that we may present every man complete in Christ"—add the element of discipleship to our definition? Or what about Matthew 28:19–20? Doesn't that passage add an element of discipleship to the definition? After all, aren't we all to make disciples?

Some might argue that we proclaim the Gospel in order that people might be effective followers of Jesus Christ. This element goes beyond the immediate intention of having a person place his trust in Jesus Christ, to the ultimate intention of having a person become a disciple of Jesus Christ.

The word *evangelism* seems to center around the proclamation of the Good News with the immediate intent that the individual will respond to the Gospel. There is no reason to minimize the importance of discipleship. Everyone should be involved in discipleship at some level. Yet the goal of evangelism is salvation. In theological terms, justification is distinct, yet not separate from sanctification. Once a person has placed his trust in Jesus Christ, then he begins the marvelous journey of sanctification, becoming more like Christ. To include the process of discipleship in the definition of evangelism expands the definition beyond the activity of proclaiming the Good News with the purpose of seeing that person respond positively to the message. Evangelism is the first mile of the road to Christlikeness.

But there are also a couple of cautions that come to mind when I define the word *evangelism*. Let's not define *evangelism* in terms of results. Let's not define *evangelism* by the number of church members or the number of contacts or converts. Typically the temptation is to measure evangelism in one's church through membership, or the number of baptisms or conversions in a given year. But I can't find any biblical basis to back that up. We must be careful not to define evangelism around some sort of result that we expect to see from sharing the Gospel.

Neither should evangelism be defined in terms of a method. It doesn't seem to say anywhere in Scripture that you have done the work of an evangelist if you have effectively used a particular tract. To base our definition of evangelism upon the effective use of a particular method would be unwise. We would be saying that evangelism has or has not taken place based upon a method rather than centered on a message. We need to be careful not to define evangelism as a method.

A DEFINITION OF EVANGELISM

The biblical definition of evangelism centers primarily on two ideas: (1) the communication of the Gospel, or the good news about Jesus Christ; and (2) the intent of inviting the listener to trust Christ.

The good news is that Jesus Christ has provided a way of salvation. Jesus Christ, because of who He is and what He has done, has provided us with a wonderful gift, a way of salvation. Sinners need a Savior, and Jesus Christ is that Savior.

Jesus Christ is the fullness of everything that we have been waiting for from the Old Testament. The Old Testament points to Him who will take away our sins. In Christ we have forgiveness of sins, the Holy Spirit, a new heart, and new life. "Behold, the Lamb of God who takes away the sin of the world!" (John 1:29). That's the Good News. Here He is! The proclamation of that good news of Jesus Christ is what evangelism is all about.

But evangelism shares the Good News so that the listener will deal with it. The listener should make some sort of decision as to what he or she is going to do with this person, Jesus Christ. "What are you going to decide to do with Jesus Christ?" Even when the listener chooses to do nothing with Jesus Christ, he or she has made a decision.

Evangelism always preaches the Gospel for the purpose of converting the listener. Evangelism's intent is that the listener will act. The messenger urges the listener to transfer his trust from all those things that he is currently trusting to what Jesus Christ has already accomplished on the Cross.

Lewis Sperry Chafer, the first president of Dallas Theological Seminary, wrote in volume 7 of his *Systematic Theology* this definition of evangelism: "Evangelism is the act of presenting to the unsaved the evangel or good news of the gospel of God's saving grace through Christ Jesus".[2] Chafer saw evangelism as an event, not a process.

> Evangelism has two main parts:
> information and invitation.

I propose a similar definition of evangelism based upon what we have discussed in this chapter. The definition I propose is:

Evangelism is the communication of the good news of Jesus Christ—that He died for our sins and rose again—with the intent of inviting the listener to trust Christ. Evangelism is telling the Good News for the purpose of inviting the sinner to salvation.

Evangelism is an event and not a process. We are to do the work of an evangelist. The definition of evangelism has two main parts: information and invitation. One part without the other is out of balance. One should not think of presenting an invitation without any information. And likewise, providing only the information without an invitation to trust Christ will leave the listener frustrated and still unsaved. After a person trusts Christ, instruction in the spiritual life starts the person down the road toward spiritual maturity.

In Figure 1, the line represents a time line of a person's life. As a person goes through life he makes a number of decisions, but eventually he comes to the place where he places his trust in Jesus Christ. Let the cross represent the moment when a person makes a decision to trust Christ as his Savior.

Figure 1
A POINT IN TIME

EVANGELISM

I have placed the word *evangelism* as an event that occurs when that individual comes to place his trust in Jesus Christ. At some point in a person's life the Good News is shared and the person responds to the message in faith.

Evangelism is an event in the midst of some process; however, I choose not to call that process the "evangelism process" due to the way that the word *evangelism* is used in Scripture. I acknowledge that there is a process involved, but calling that process the "evangelism process" goes past the way the word *evangelism* is used in Scripture. Evangelism centers around the proclamation of the good news about Jesus Christ.

You make the call. When does evangelism take place? None of those scenarios introduced at the beginning of the chapter was "evangelism." In all of those scenarios I was being a good witness in one sense or another, but the Gospel was not proclaimed.

In each of those scenarios, as a witness I was building a bridge for the Gospel to be shared. But evangelism itself is the communication of the good news about Jesus Christ with the intent of inviting the listener to trust Christ. Evangelism focuses around the proclamation of the message.

Is this merely semantics? Possibly; however, definitions are important because definitions determine behavior. How I define terms determines how I will live. If I define evangelism very broadly, the danger is that everything in life becomes "evangelism" and the message may never be communicated. However, evangelism in Scripture focuses around the proclamation of the Good News. How you define evangelism will affect how you carry out the task that has been assigned to every believer.

Have you taken liberty with the definition of evangelism? How has that definition affected your behavior?

THREE:
HOW DOES THIS ALL FIT TOGETHER?

EVANGELISM PRINCIPLE 2: *Evangelism is an event in the process of disciple making.*

MY SON TIM received his first model car at Christmas many years ago. He was excited as he unwrapped the paper that revealed a nice red Porsche on the box top. Never having seen a model before, he expected to open up that box and find inside a nice, shiny red car just like the one in the picture on the box top. Unfortunately, when he opened the package all he found were green plastic pieces awaiting his assembly.

He was disappointed, but he faced still another dilemma: How did this thing all fit together? He was determined to assemble this car, but where did all the pieces go? I was able to introduce him to the assembly directions that came with the model, and he was off and running with painstaking work.

In the previous chapter we defined evangelism as the communication of the good news of Jesus Christ with the intent of inviting the listener to trust Christ. But we too are faced with still another dilemma. The word *evangelism* has been used a variety of different ways. It has been used to try to describe a number of different strategies of evangelism. How does this all fit together? We have opened the box of defining evangelism, yet we are left staring at a box of pieces.

How does this definition help me sort out all the different evangelistic strategies? Am I saying that just living a good life is not evangelism? Am I saying that mowing my neighbor's yard is not evangelism?

That is exactly what I am saying. We will be looking further at this distinction a little later in the book. However, to begin to sort out all of the pieces it is helpful to look at the way the term *evangelism* is used today.

The term *evangelism* is being used today to try to describe a number of different strategies. Recognize that *a strategy of evangelism* is the means by which evangelism takes place. A strategy is a bridge so that the message can be shared. Unfortunately, when we use the term *evangelism* to describe a particular strategy, often the term *evangelism* is equated with a strategy. The strategy that we employ to share the Gospel is not evangelism. The strategy is a vehicle for evangelism to take place. Below are different strategies that the term *evangelism* has been used to try to describe.

PROCLAMATIONAL EVANGELISM STRATEGY

Proclamational evangelism strategy focuses on presenting the Gospel in a context where a large number of listeners are present and are exposed to the truth. The context in which the truth is presented becomes a primary factor in this strategy. As with any strategy, there are pros and cons.

Proclamational evangelism has many benefits. It is biblical. Examples of this strategy being used might be Peter in Jerusalem (Acts 2:14–36) or Philip in Samaria (Acts 8:5), Paul in Lystra (Acts 14:6–7) or Paul with the Athenians (Acts 17:16–34). Often there are large audiences with one person proclaiming the Gospel. Therefore the evangelist is reaching a large number of people at that one time with the proclamation of the Gospel.

On the downside, proclamational evangelism strategies can be impersonal. You don't really have a personal time of sitting down with an individual who might be up on the 66th row. In fact, it is nearly impossible to really understand where that individual on the 66th row might be in the process of everything happening in his or her life. You really do not have the opportunity to understand that individual's hurts, fears, or questions. It's a one-way conversation. However, the strategy itself is an effective vehicle for evangelism to take place.

AGGRESSIVE EVANGELISM STRATEGY

Aggressive evangelism strategy focuses on the message of the gospel of Jesus Christ and confronting the listener with the decision that must be made in response. The confrontation and call for a decision becomes a primary factor. An example of this strategy in practice would be Philip with the Ethiopian eunuch on the Gaza road in Acts 8:26–40. Jesus provided the supreme example as He met with Zaccheus (Luke 19:1–10), Nicodemus (John 3:1–21), and the woman at the well (John 4:1–42). He was always spending time with the sick, the less fortunate, the Pharisees, and sinners. He had direct contact with individuals like the rich young ruler and the unnamed woman in Luke 7:36–50.

Aggressive evangelism strategy has also been referred to as confrontational or intrusional evangelism. What types of activities are we talking about when we talk about aggressive strategies of evangelism? Door-to-door evangelism might be more aggressive in nature. Any activity that focuses on sharing the Gospel with a call for a decision may be considered aggressive.

There are some benefits that are associated with aggressive strategies. There's a sense of urgency that's communicated. Aggressive strategies are usually transferable. And there is interaction that's going on between the speaker and the listener, making it more personal.

However, there are also some drawbacks with aggressive strategies. The presentation could come across as being canned or insensitive rather than being personal. It could also come across, depending upon how it is presented, as obnoxious or offensive. However, these strategies need not be obnoxious or offensive. It really depends on how one views people.

RELATIONAL EVANGELISM STRATEGY

Relational evangelism strategy focuses on bringing a person along in the process to a place where the Gospel is shared as a natural result of the relationship that has developed over a period of time. The relationship between people becomes a primary factor. Paul demonstrates a relational strategy as he ministers to the Thessalonians in 1 Thessalonians 2:1–12.

There are some positives associated with relational strategies. Hopefully, there is more of the demonstration of the Gospel through one's walk, rather than one's words alone. A relationship is built between presenter and unbeliever. Time is not a factor. There's not much of a rush with relational types of things.

A lot of sensitivity is built between the two individuals. Hopefully the presenter has more of an idea of what's going on in the listener's mind, where the hurts are, the fears are, and is able to diagnose a lot better the individual's needs. The Gospel can then be presented in light of the listener's needs and his situation in life.

You've established a relationship. Consequently, after that person places his trust in Jesus Christ there is that dynamic, which has him already started down the road toward discipleship, which will continue in the future.

What are some of the drawbacks? The sense of urgency present in aggressive strategies might be lost in the relationship. The time element has been set aside, so urgency is not as high a priority.

There might be a loss of focus. The emphasis might become more the friendship or the relationship rather than the evangelism or the actual proclamation of the Good News. Until the Gospel is actually presented, evangelism has not truly occurred. It is good to keep in mind that all relational strategies must become aggressive at some point; otherwise, that person is still lost.

If we add these definitions to our chart that we began in the last chapter, then our chart will begin to fill out as in Figure 2. Because of the way that the word *evangelism* is used, it is sometimes used to describe a number of different strategies.

Figure 2
EVANGELISM STRATEGIES

EVANGELISM

1. Proclamational Strategy
2. Aggressive Strategy
3. Relational Strategy

THE RELATIONSHIP BETWEEN TWO STRATEGIES

The evangelical community today has put the term *evangelism* on two ends of a continuum. We seem to have created a dichotomy between two different types of strategies. At the one end of the continuum we have relational strategies, with a number of people writing from that perspective.[1] And at the other end of the spectrum we have aggressive strategies, with writers championing that particular evangelistic activity.

Relational strategy	Aggressive strategy
(Rely more on your walk and emphasize cultivation)	(Rely more on your talk and emphasize harvesting)

The people in the relational-strategy camp talk a lot about the cultivation and talk little about the harvest. The writers in the aggressive-strategy camp talk a lot about the harvest, but talk little about the cultivation. Normally a person has to choose between one of the two strategies.

It seems to me that both are correct, if properly employed. We ought to target some sort of middle ground where we see the two united with such terms as *cultivation, sowing,* and *harvesting.* There is a proper time for cultivation, a proper time for sowing, and a proper time for harvesting.

On occasion I hear individuals state categorically, "I am a relational, or lifestyle, evangelist!" I should hope so. There are times when we all should be involved in a "lifestyle" strategy of evangelism. There needs to be a time of cultivation. If it's cultivation we are talking about when we talk about relational strategies, then we are on the right track. Cultivation is absolutely necessary. But all cultivation with no harvest leaves the person without any resolution to his or her problem with sin.

There comes a time when we need to sow verbal seeds. There comes a time when we need to provide some value statements. But there also comes a time for harvesting. "Christianity is enshrined in the life: but it is proclaimed by the lips," noted Michael Green.[2] We are witnesses by our very lives, but we are each to do the work of an evangelist.

BEING A WITNESS

I am a volunteer chaplain at a couple of local hospitals. Every week I donate a few hours to minister to those who are suffering. If I go to the hospital and am there merely as a presence, is that evangelism? No, I am a witness. I am a witness by who I am.

Acts 1:8 reads, "You will receive power when the Holy Spirit has come upon you; and you shall be My witnesses both in Jerusalem, and in all Judea and Samaria, and even to the remotest part of the earth." Because of the indwelling presence of the Holy Spirit, I am a witness for Jesus Christ. In the book of Acts the disciples were witnesses specifically of the resurrection of Jesus Christ. They were able to bear testimony of the Resurrection. In the same fashion, the indwelling Holy Spirit enables us to testify to the resurrected Christ.

Being a witness is good and valuable, but I also need to "do the work of an evangelist" (2 Timothy 4:5). Doing the work of an evangelist is doing the work of one who announces or proclaims the Good News that Jesus Christ died for my sins and arose from the dead. When I have the opportunity to proclaim the gospel of Jesus Christ and invite a response, I am involved in evangelism. I can be a witness and not do the work of an evangelist.

There are different types of ways that I can be a witness for Jesus Christ. I can have a life witness where my life serves as a witness for Jesus Christ. How I live and how I conduct myself become a witness for the Lord. That witness can be a good witness, or it can be a bad witness. But because of the indwelling of the Holy Spirit in my life, my life is a witness for the Lord.

I can also have a verbal witness for the Lord. I can give testimony for what the Lord has done in my life. When I give a testimony for the Lord, is that evangelism? No, it is a verbal witness. I might say, "God is good." That is true, and that is a good statement about God, but it is not the Gospel. It is a verbal testimony to God's goodness.

We also have a corporate witness for the Lord. How we treat each other is a witness to the outside world. By the way that we treat each other, we can have a good witness or we can have a bad witness. Jesus said, "By this all men will know that you are My disciples, if you have love for one another" (John 13:35).

If we add those categories to our chart, we have something that looks like Figure 3. Being a witness is being salt and light in the world. However, we have been called to do the work of an evangelist.

Figure 3
THE WITNESS THAT PRECEDES EVANGELISM

WITNESS	EVANGELISM
1. Life	1. Proclamational Strategy
2. Verbal	2. Aggressive Strategy
3. Corporate	3. Relational Strategy
"Salt and Light"	"Do the work of an evangelist"

Cultivation	Sowing	Harvesting

IS THERE A PROCESS INVOLVED?

Doesn't a person come to Christ over a period of time? Sometimes, but not always. But if a period of time is involved, what is the most accurate or precise term to describe that process? Is that process to be defined as an evangelism process?

I would say that process is not biblical evangelism. The word *evangelism* revolves around the proclamation of the Good News. Is it a witness process? No. Witnessing is who I am. I am a testimony of something that has happened in my life.

> How we live serves as a foundation
> for evangelism, not as a substitute.

I would prefer to call the process the *disciple-making* process (see Figure 4).[3] In Matthew 28:16–20, Jesus calls us to "go therefore and make disciples of all the nations" (verse 19). The command in that sentence is "make disciples." Three participles modify "make disciples": go, baptizing (v. 19), and teaching (v. 20). There is a process involved in making a disciple. Part of that process of making a disciple is evangelism; however, notice that the process continues after the person believes in Jesus Christ as one becomes involved in discipleship or follow-up. (The role of follow-up in the disciple-making process is detailed in chapter 15.)

Figure 4

THE DISCIPLE-MAKING PROCESS

WITNESS	EVANGELISM	FOLLOW-UP
1. Life	1. Proclamational Strategy	
2. Verbal	2. Aggressive Strategy	
3. Corporate	3. Relational Strategy	
"Salt and Light"	"Do the work of an evangelist"	
Cultivation	Sowing	Harvesting

All evangelism is a form of witnessing, but not all witnessing is a form of evangelism. How we live serves as a foundation for evangelism, not as a substitute. One of the dangers in the disciple-making process is to deceive ourselves by thinking that giving a verbal witness of God's faithfulness (or something else) in our life is evangelism.

When I look at "evangelism" in the Scriptures, the word revolves around the proclamation of the good news about Jesus Christ. How we live, and the things that we do, serve as a foundation for evangelism to take place. How we live is not a substitute for evangelism.

> We are to love the unlovely ...
> and get involved in their lives.

We need to get involved in people's lives. Time for building and cultivation of interpersonal relationships is vital. We are to love the unlovely. Be genuine and get involved in their lives. There is a time for giving a verbal witness to what Christ has done in your life. There is also a time of harvesting, of sharing with them the good news of Jesus Christ.

A lot of people use the term *evangelism* in a very broad sense, saying that almost any activity for Christ is included in evangelism. But that is going beyond the way the term *evangelism* is used in Scripture. Scripture seems to focus evangelism on the proclamation of the Good News.

Making friends with an individual is good. But unless that person comes to a place where he knows and trusts Jesus Christ, he is still lost! We need to keep that distinction very clear. Evangelism is an event of sharing with someone the opportunity to transfer his trust from himself and his own effort to Jesus Christ and His saving effort on his behalf. Unless this personal transfer of trust occurs, a person is still lost and unsaved. Being the friend of the most dynamic Christian around is of no spiritual benefit unless a transfer of faith to Jesus Christ takes place. A person will not make it to heaven on the basis of merit, but only through a personal relationship with Jesus Christ.

Evangelism needs to take place some time. There may have been a lot of cultivation going on, there may be a lot of sowing going on, but still there needs to be a transformation for that lost person to become a believer.

YOU MAKE THE CALL

Evangelism principle number two is: Evangelism is an event in the process of disciple making. You make the call. Are you involved in doing the work of an evangelist? How have you been using the term "evangelism"? Has your life primarily been characterized by being a good witness for Jesus Christ, but not by doing the work of an evangelist? You can be the greatest witness, but if you never get around to sharing the Gospel, the person is still lost.

Think clearly about your personal strategy. Put some balance back in your evangelistic life.

FOUR:
HOW OPEN ARE YOU?

MY PARENTS LIVE in Colorado. A few winters ago, around Christmas, we decided to take the family to Colorado to enjoy some winter activities. One of the activities we decided to experience as a family was a snowmobiling excursion.

The entire "Cecil" crew (which included part of my brother's clan) took up seven snowmobiles. We outfitted ourselves with snowmobile suits, helmets, mittens, and boots, and off we went motoring through the woods. It was exhilarating! The snow, the mountains, the woods were all great. We did everything that tourists were supposed to do.

On the way back to the shack, however, we encountered a blizzard. It was the worst snowfall that I have ever experienced. I came to understand the meaning of the word *whiteout*. The flakes came fast and thick. I could barely see the snowmobile in front of ours, even though it was only a few feet ahead and had a red taillight.

In fact, the snowfall got so bad the red light was all that I could see. It was everything that I could do to focus on that light ahead of me. My priority was not to lose that light.

Picture in your mind white surrounding you with a dim, fuzzy, red light going in and out of your sight. The moments that you lose sight of that light, you become fearful of being separated from the rest of the group and lost in the woods. Words that have been used in our family to try to express that very experience are *scared, cold, tired,* and *focused.*

We successfully made it back to the shack. But the story still circulates.

That memory gives me new insight into the phrase "staying focused." My concentration was high. All I could remember saying to myself along the trail was, *Keep your eye on the light. That light is the only way home.*

In this situation, being focused was the only way to go. On the other hand, sometimes we can become *too* focused. That happens in evangelism. We can become too focused on only one strategy, or one way, to share the Gospel. How open are you to attempting new strategies to reach people with the Gospel? Have you already predetermined your approach? Have you already determined what you will and will not attempt for God?

The Bible records a number of different strategies utilized in the early church. In this chapter, I would like to look at some of the ways that the Bible teaches that the Gospel was being spread in the early church. This list is not intended to be exhaustive but should expand our horizons a bit.[1]

HOSPITALITY IN THE HOME

One of the most important methods of spreading the Gospel in antiquity was through the use of homes. In Acts 2:46–47 we read, "Day by day continuing with one mind in the temple, and breaking bread *from house to house,* they were taking their meals together with gladness and sincerity of heart, praising God and having favor with all the people. And the Lord was adding to their number day by day those who were being saved" (italics added).

Lydia's house in Philippi (Acts 16:15) was used for hospitality. Philip's house at Caesarea also seems to have been open for hospitality (Acts 21:8). At least Paul stayed there, and Philip is the only person in the New Testament who is specifically mentioned as an evangelist.

Have you ever considered using your home as a place for hospitality and evangelism? Paul says in Romans 12:13 Christians are to be "practicing hospitality." There are many advantages to using your home. The main advantage is that the visitor is on your turf! There is a natural informality and a relaxed atmosphere in the home. It provides a natural arena for conversation and interaction between participants. The bottom line is that you have the opportunity to relax and get to know your guest.

Why is it that we always think of evangelism as taking place somewhere else? I am often confronted with the complaint, "I do not have any opportunities to come into contact with unbelievers." My reply is very simple, "Do you eat?" If you eat, you have the opportunity to demonstrate hospitality to someone. Invite your neighbor over for dinner! It does not need to be anything fancy; it just needs to be genuine and authentic hospitality.

You have the opportunity to extend hospitality to your neighbors just by inviting them over for pizza. It is a great way to get to know them, and it is a great way to explore with them their relationship with Christ. "Tell me about yourself" is a great opening. Talk about their background. Talk about their work and their family. Once you have explored those interests you might merely ask, "Are you interested in spiritual things?" Or you might just ask, "May I ask you a spiritual question?"

Remember also that everyone that you come in contact with is a link to another person. The concept of the "household" in Scripture is vitally important. It was the Philippian jailer and his whole household who came to the Lord (Acts 16:33). Just because you are talking to one individual does not mean that other people are not impacted or involved.

When I go into a hospital room, I am primarily there for the patient; however, I need to realize that the family needs ministry as well.

To ignore or neglect the family would be to miss an opportunity. Needy people are needy people no matter where they may be.

What about you? Have you considered using your home as a vehicle to demonstrate hospitality and share the Gospel? Or are you looking at evangelism in only one way? Have you already determined that evangelism only takes place somewhere else? Are you willing to be used by God to explore this option?

PROCLAMATION IN RELIGIOUS CENTERS

In the early church, the Gospel was being shared through hospitality in the home and also through proclamation. The Gospel was being proclaimed in a number of different places and in a number of different ways.

First, the Gospel was being proclaimed in the religious centers of the day. Paul's strategy to proclaim the Gospel in a city was to first go into the synagogue. In fact, in Acts 17:2 we read, "And according to Paul's custom, he went to them" in the synagogue. Paul was continually found speaking in the synagogues: in Salamis, in Pisidian Antioch, in Iconium, in Thessalonica, in Berea, in Athens, in Corinth, and in Ephesus.[2]

In the religious center Paul was found reasoning from the Scriptures and "explaining and giving evidence that the Christ had to suffer and rise again from the dead" (Acts 17:3). The apostle, in speaking in those religious centers, already had an audience that was interested in spiritual matters.

Obviously, the Gospel should be boldly proclaimed today through the churches. Whatever church, Bible study, or organization that you may be a part of provides the opportunity to share the Gospel. During national crises or tragedies, churches are full. People continue to seek refuge and answers from God. Have you assumed that everyone in your study is already a believer? Are you open to exploring the topic of the Gospel in your group?

PROCLAMATION THROUGH
OPEN-AIR PREACHING

Jesus was a master of open-air preaching. The Sermon on the Mount is a great example of open-air preaching. While Jesus begins to teach the disciples (Matthew 5:1–2) the "crowds were amazed" (Matthew 7:28). Jesus was always involved in preaching to the people who were nearby. Jesus would take advantage of any opportunity to proclaim the Good News, or teach truths about the kingdom. Other examples of open-air preaching might be Peter in Jerusalem, or Philip in Samaria, or Paul in Athens (in Acts 2:14ff; 8:5; 17:22–33).

In each instance, the speaker chose to preach where a number of people either gathered or passed by. Today we might see this duplicated by preaching on a street corner or in some other public arena.

Perhaps you have already dismissed open-air preaching as an option in your life. Pause here. Have you already said in your heart, "I will not be involved in that!"? *Now* we are getting down to exploring just how open you are. If you are at the place where you have already dismissed open-air preaching as an option for the communication of the Gospel, then you are just like Jonah!

Jonah, when asked by God to go to Nineveh, told God an emphatic *no.* In essence, he was shaking his fist at God. He was not relying upon God to be able to use him in that situation. Jonah decided that he knew better than God and headed toward Tarshish. Unfortunately, Jonah was in for a whale of a learning experience. At the bottom of Jonah's heart was a spirit of independence and arrogance.

It is one thing to be open to God's leading and quite another thing to have already decided in advance that you are not going to do something. It is one thing to be dependent upon God to provide the necessary resources to go where He calls and quite another thing to think that you know better than God.

How open are you to exploring where God might be leading in

your life? Would you be willing to explore open-air preaching as an option if God called?

PROCLAMATION THROUGH TEACHING AND APOLOGETICS

Paul was obviously known for his apologetics. "Apologetics may be defined as the clarification and defense of the total system of biblical Christianity."[3]

Paul's apologetics were so powerful that he had to defend himself before Felix about his actions in Jerusalem. His accusers found Paul "a real pest and a fellow who sirs up dissension among all the Jews through-out the world, and a ringleader of the sect of the Nazarenes" (Acts 24:5). During his response Paul said, "Neither in the temple, nor in the synagogues, nor in the city itself did they find me carrying on a discussion with anyone or causing a riot" (v. 12). When was the last time that you were accused of starting a riot as a result of preaching the Gospel?

Paul was "reasoning" with the Jews in the synagogue and with the Gentiles in the marketplace every day in Athens (Acts 17:17). When Paul was in Ephesus he "reason[ed] daily in the school of Tyrannus" (Acts 19:9). In fact, this was so effective over the two plus years that he was there that "some of the Asiarchs who were friends of his sent to him and repeatedly urged him not to venture into the theater" (Acts 19:31) due to the possible disturbance.

Are you "ready to make a defense to everyone who asks you to give an account for the hope that is in you" (1 Peter 3:15)? Have you been equipped to be able to "contend earnestly for the faith" (Jude 3)?

Is apologetics available in your toolbox to be used if God calls upon it to be used? Or have you already established that this is one area that you are not interested in pursuing?

Please note, however, that apologetics is a bridge for the Gospel to be shared. Apologetics is not the Gospel. We will explore this truth in detail in chapter 14.

It seems that for most people, though, apologetics has fallen on tough times. "Maybe they will ask me a question that I do not know!" Let me encourage you: They probably *will* ask you a question that you do not know the answer to. But in most communication it is not so much what you know, but how you say it. If you see the person the way God sees that person, and love that person the way God loves that person, then you will be able to get away with a lot. You may not have all of the answers, but the way you respond to them in love will win them over every time.

How open are you to be used by God in this area? I am not asking you if you are going to be used in this area, or if you are qualified to be used in this area; I am asking you, How open are you to being used by God in this area? Or have you already told God that you are not interested?

PROCLAMATION THROUGH TESTIMONY

The testimony of the apostles was one of the most powerful tools available to proclaim the Gospel. The apostles prior to the Resurrection were a motley crowd who scattered when asked if they were with the man from Galilee. Peter even denied his Lord three times on that night in which Jesus was betrayed. However, after the Resurrection, each one became a zealot for Jesus Christ. Their lives had changed, giving testimony to the work of God in them.

Paul gives a wonderful testimony to the power of God in his life beginning in 2 Corinthians 11. In fact, Paul would write to Timothy: "It is a trustworthy statement, deserving full acceptance, that Christ Jesus came into the world to save sinners, among whom I am foremost of all" (1 Timothy 1:15). The testimony is how God saves sinners! Paul's personal testimony in Philippians 3 is a great example that he uses effectively to clarify works versus faith.

Other testimonies are used to encourage the believers, as Paul uses the church in Macedonia to encourage the Corinthians in their giving

(2 Corinthians 8:1–8). Or testimonies are used to encourage us in ministry to not lose heart (2 Corinthians 4).

Other testimonies are faith stories telling of how God has worked in the past. Stephen starts with how God appeared to Abraham and then tells the story of the nation of Israel (Acts 7:2–53). When the nation heard that they were just like their fathers (Acts 7:51), they stoned Stephen.

Paul uses the same strategy as he talks with the "men of Israel" (Acts 13:16) in the synagogue in Pisidian Antioch. Paul starts with how God led the nation out of Egypt and ends with the resurrection of Jesus Christ (Acts 13:16–41).

In both cases God's grace and goodness is given testimony through faith stories of the past. Faith stories of how God has worked in your life are powerful tools in God's hands. Are you open to share those stories?

PERSONAL EVANGELISM

While the public proclamation was crucial in the spread of the Gospel, no less important was personal evangelism. The Gospel was being shared through personal encounters with individuals.

We mentioned in the last chapter that Jesus provided the supreme example of personal evangelism as He met with Zaccheus (Luke 19:1–10), Nicodemus (John 3:1–21), and the woman at the well (John 4:1–42). But consider also the direct contact that Jesus had with people like Mary and Martha, Lazarus, the disciples, or the rich young ruler.

Jesus also had a number of personal encounters with people through healing. Consider the paralytic man lowered through the roof in Capernaum (Mark 2:1–12). Or consider the man with the withered hand (Mark 3:1–6), the demon-possessed man in the country of the Gerasenes (Mark 5:1–20), the hemorrhaging woman (Mark 5:25–34), or the blind man in Bethsaida (Mark 8:22–26). In all of these examples, Jesus practiced personal contact with people and pointed them toward the spiritual through the physical.

Other personal evangelistic encounters in Scripture included Philip on the Gaza road with the Ethiopian eunuch (Acts 8:26–40) and Peter and John with the lame man by the temple (Acts 3:1–10). The personal encounter of Paul with the Philippian jailer ended with the jailer crying out, "What must I do to be saved?" (Acts 16:30).

All of these personal encounters included broader relationships. It is good to keep in mind that there were many other people that were touched through the initial encounter with these folks. When Jesus spoke with the paralytic man lowered through the roof in Capernaum, the four men who carried that pallet to the roof and lowered that man through the roof were impacted by the sight. After John the Baptist proclaimed Jesus as the Lamb of God to the two disciples (John 1:35–37), one of them, Andrew, brought his brother Simon (Peter) to Christ (John 1:40–43). And after Jesus found Philip (John 1:43), Philip found Nathanael and brought him to Jesus (John 1:45ff).

> The key is to love people
> the way that God loves people.

Paul referred to some of the people whom he wrote about as his children. While they might have come to know the Lord by another method, the personal nature of the reference leads the reader to assume that there was a personal relationship involved (e.g., Paul with Timothy).

How open are you to being involved in personal encounters with individuals? Today we seem to have associated personal evangelism, or the aggressive strategy of evangelism, with being obnoxious and offensive. There is nothing in Scripture to suggest that aggressive strategies need to be offensive and obnoxious. The key is to love people the way that God loves people. You are not going to be able to love people like that in the flesh. It is a spiritual thing.

Are personal encounters with individuals a possibility in your thinking, or have you already decided that you are not going to be involved in this way?

LITERARY EVANGELISM

In addition to speaking about Christ, the early church also wrote about Christ. Literary evangelism was also open to the early church to communicate the Good News to a lost world. Obviously Scripture had a big part in the spread of the Gospel. John even explained that he wrote his gospel narrative "that you may believe that Jesus is the Christ, the Son of God; and that believing you may have life in His name" (John 20:31).

The Word of God is "living and active and sharper than any two-edged sword" (Hebrews 4:12) and is able "to give you the wisdom that leads to salvation through faith which is in Christ Jesus" (2 Timothy 3:15). Scripture also encourages believers to pray and be bold in evangelism (Ephesians 6:18–20).

Anybody can be involved in evangelism through literature. Letters, tracts, and articles are all opportunities to share the Gospel with an unbeliever.

Is sharing the Gospel through literature an option for you? Or have you already decided that the use of literature in evangelism is not your style?

ARE STYLES A MATTER
OF PERSONAL PREFERENCE?

Is my evangelism strategy just a matter of personal preference? Is it up to me to choose which style fits best?

I once attended a conference where the leaders were discussing various styles of evangelism. A number of different styles were presented, and attendees could easily have received the impression that one may pick his or her particular style of evangelism. Whatever was comfortable for you was perfectly all right. All you needed to do was to find the approach that fit you.

As the conference went on, most of the attendees decided that the relational strategy of evangelism was for them. In fact, an informal survey during the conference confirmed that was the favored personal approach. Furthermore, the relational style was the style that the seminar leader felt the most comfortable with as well.

One of the older gentlemen at the back of the room raised his hand and asked the leader, "Sir, if we all decided that the best way to be able to reach our neighborhood for Jesus Christ was to go door-to-door, would you join us?" The leader's answer stunned me. "No, I wouldn't," he said. "That is just not my style." That leader was focused more on himself and his preference than on other people and their needs.

God tends to choose and use
people outside their comfort zones.

One of the problems with taking evangelism inventories is that you record your preference on the inventory. Everywhere in Scripture I see that God uses people outside their preferences. I would imagine that if we were to give Moses an inventory, he would have said that his preference was to remain in the land of Midian and be a shepherd. Midian is where he felt the most comfortable. However, God had a different plan for Moses. God was calling him to lead His people out of the land of Egypt.

Even when God revealed what He had in mind, Moses began to argue with God. "Who am I, that I should go to Pharaoh, and that I should bring the sons of Israel out of Egypt? . . . What if they will not believe me or listen to what I say? . . . Please, Lord, I have never been eloquent, neither recently nor in time past, nor since You have spoken to Your servant; for I am slow of speech and slow of tongue" (Exodus 3:11; 4:1, 10). God even knew that Aaron, Moses' brother, was more eloquent (Exodus 4:14), but God chose Moses as His spokesman.

In Scripture, God tends to choose and use people outside their comfort zones. Maybe it is to keep us dependent upon Him. How open are you to be used by God in a place where you do not feel adequate?

Have you already decided what you will and will not do for the Lord? Whenever I hear people state boldly, "I am into relational strategies!" or "I am into aggressive strategies!" the thought running through my head is, "Wow, that is selfish!" You see, every sentence they use is beginning with "I" or "Me." Instead of seeing a person in the way that God sees a person, or loving a person the way that God loves the person, we begin to inflict our preferences on people. Instead of asking, What is best for this person? our natural tendency is to ask, What is best for me? Instead of being available to be used of God to communicate the Gospel in the best way to an individual, we are only looking at ourselves and what we feel comfortable with.

Evangelism is not about you! It is all about God. It is all about His grace. You are merely the vessel that God has chosen to use to communicate His message.

HOW OPEN ARE YOU?

Although this brief examination of Scripture is not exhaustive or complete, it is designed to ask the question, How open are you? Have you already decided what you will and will not participate in?

The above quick survey of Scripture does not even take into account the opportunities that we have through media. Today we are able to present the Gospel through television, radio, video, or electronic means, including the Internet! Are you open to the possibility of how God might use you in these endeavors?

So, how open are you? May we be so open and so equipped to be able to be used by God in whatever way He sees fit.

FIVE:
WHY GO ACROSS THE STREET?

THE CHURCH WAS right across the street from a state university that housed twelve thousand students. In fact, if you walked out the front door of the church and crossed the street, you would enter one of the academic buildings on campus.

In talking with the elders of the church about possible ways to reach out to that college campus, I encountered a very basic argument that is not too uncommon in today's thinking. The argument was voiced by one of the men present and went something like this: "Why do we need to go across the street? We have a nice steeple, a nice white fence, and even a sign that indicates when our services are held. If anybody is interested in joining us, they are more than welcome. In fact, if we leave the front doors open on Sunday morning, they will be able to hear us singing! Why do we need to go across the street?"

Now before you criticize this gentleman too much, remember that this argument is not too far from some current thinking. "Why do I need to actually talk to somebody about Jesus Christ? If I just live my life in a godly way, won't they ask me about my personal relationship with Jesus Christ? Why do I need to purposefully engage the unbeliever?"

"Why do I need to go across the street?" they question.

This little scenario also raises another question. What is our motivation for evangelism? Is evangelism merely a duty—one more item on my "to do" list? Should I lead people into making a commitment to Christ so I can say I have done my evangelistic duty?

The answer really is found in Scripture. The question posed by that elder encouraged a small group Bible study designed to answer the question, "Why go across the street?"

HOW DO YOU VIEW THE FATHER?

Evangelism has everything to do with the Father. So in order to answer the question, Why go across the street to evangelize? let's consider who the Father really is.

The greatest motivator for world evangelization is based in the character of God. How you view the Father is directly related to your walk with Him—and it affects what Father you are communicating to a lost world. What does the Father whom you are holding out to a lost world look like?

Perhaps you view the Father as someone who is disappointed with you; if so, that may be the Father you are holding out to a lost world. Or perhaps you view the Father as someone who is very distant and uninterested in you; if so, you may present the Father as someone who couldn't care less about our personal issues. What kind of hope does that hold out to a lost world?

Some view the Father as some sort of cosmic inspector, who is always looking over their shoulders to see if they measure up to the rules, standards, and regulations. When they get up in the morning, the first thing they say is, "I have to have a quiet time." Afterward, they check it off their list, as if completing the task has fulfilled their duty, earning them some sort of spiritual points with God. What are the implications of presenting the Lord that way to the lost?

Others see the Father as someone who is delighted to spend some time with them. He is a person who is an intimate friend, who cares deeply about them and what they are thinking. Do you see a warm, compassionate, and caring Father who is excited and passionate to get to know you? Do you see a Father who is passionate about reconciliation because of His great love and concern for you? Who could resist a Father like that?

What kind of Father do you communicate to a lost world? Who would want to respond to an angry, distant, and disinterested Father? Our Father has a heart for the lost.

THE FATHER'S HEART

Why go across the street? The answer is, Because it is a reflection of the Father's heart. But now the question broadens a little and we have to ask another question: What does the Father's heart look like? If the reason that we should go across the street is because it is a reflection of the Father's heart, then what does the Father's pulse and heartbeat look like?

If we are becoming more and more conformed to the image of Jesus Christ, then what characteristics should be emerging in our lives? If the Holy Spirit dwells within us and through the power of the Holy Spirit we are being sanctified, then how should that look in the life of the believer?

To answer those questions, let's look at Scripture. There are many characteristics of the Father's heart. All of the attributes of the Father should be becoming a part of our lives; however, three stand out when it comes to our desire to go across the street. I believe that the Father's heart is expressed in three ways: a concern for the world, a compassion for the lost, and a passion for reconciliation.

A CONCERN FOR THE WORLD

The first characteristic of the Father's heart is that He has a concern for the world. Whatever you would like to say about the Great

Commission passages, one thing you have to agree upon is that the Father has a concern for the world.

In Matthew 28:18–20 we have what is called the Great Commission passage. The eleven disciples had gone to Galilee, "to the mountain which Jesus had designated. When they saw Him, they worshiped Him; but some were doubtful" (Matthew 28:16–17).

Some worshiped, but some were doubtful. This is encouraging to me. They were normal people, with normal fears and normal doubts. The word for *doubtful* is the Greek word *distazo,* which means "to stand in two ways (*dis,* double, *stasis,* a standing), implying uncertainty about which way to take."[1] You can almost hear the confusion in the word. Some worshiped, but some were *distazo*—they had an uncertain faith.

Jesus knew what His disciples were going through. He knew they were wrestling with His departure. But it is interesting to note that our Savior did not stand around and talk about their fears or their doubts. Instead of a dialogue about their fears, Jesus proceeded to give them the Great Commission. He proceeded to give them their marching orders.

In presenting this Great Commission, Jesus underlines a very important concept in evangelism. *Our doubt will be dispelled through obedience to God's commands.* Jesus knows our doubts and our fears, but if you want to deal with your doubts and your fears, be obedient! As you are obedient to what God has called you to do, your doubts will be dispelled. As you step out in faith, God will meet you at your point of deepest fear.

Jesus gives His disciples the Great Commission: "And Jesus came up and spoke to them, saying, 'All authority has been given to Me in heaven and on earth. Go therefore and make disciples of all the nations, baptizing them in the name of the Father and the Son and the Holy Spirit, teaching them to observe all that I commanded you; and lo, I am with you always, even to the end of the age'" (Matthew 28:18–20).

Jesus tells His disciples, "All authority has been given to Me." Jesus has the authority in heaven and on earth. What comfort! At the end of the passage, Jesus reinforces this concept and gives further comfort and encouragement when He states, "I am with you always, even to the end of the age."

We are not going to be called to do anything that our Lord has not given us the resources to accomplish. He has all the authority, and He is going to be with us! In effect, Jesus says, "I am not sending you across the street by yourself. I will be with you."

Second, Jesus says to the Twelve, "Make disciples!" The phrase "make disciples" is all one word in the Greek, and it is in the imperative tense. In other words, Jesus says, "This is what I want you to do! Go and make disciples!"

There are three participles that surround the imperative "make disciples," go, baptizing, and teaching. The participles describe the method of making disciples.[2]

But the point that I would like to highlight from the text is what Jesus says next to the Twelve. He wants them to make disciples "of all the nations." No matter what you want to say about the Great Commission, you have to come away with the thought that God has a heart for the world.

Other passages that mention the Great Commission all carry with them the notion that God has a heart for the world. In Mark 16:15, we are to preach "to all creation." In Luke 24:47, we are to preach forgiveness of sins "to all the nations." In Acts 1:8, Jesus said that we will be His witnesses "to the remotest part of the earth."

Other passages also indicate God's heart for the world. Isaiah 49:6b reads, "I will also make you a light of the nations so that My salvation may reach to the end of the earth." Psalm 67:2 reads, "That Your way may be known on the earth, Your salvation among all nations." If you only say one thing about all of these passages, what you would have to say is that God has a heart for the world.

Why do we go across the street? Because it is a reflection of the Father's heart. What does the Father's heart look like? First, He has a heart for the world.

A COMPASSION FOR THE LOST

Not only does the Father have a heart for the world, but He also has a compassion for the lost. In Matthew 9:36–38 we see Jesus reacting to the people. We read, "Seeing the [multitudes], He felt compassion for them, because they were distressed and dispirited like sheep without a shepherd. Then He said to His disciples, 'The harvest is plentiful, but the workers are few. Therefore beseech the Lord of the harvest to send out workers into His harvest.'"

Biblical compassion always
has a resulting action … mercy.

As Jesus saw the multitudes, He felt compassion for them. It is interesting that as you look at the meaning of the word *compassion* in Scripture, biblical compassion encompasses a resulting action. "Compassion is so identifying with another's need that we are compelled to meet it," notes missionary Jeffery L. Townsend.[3] Biblical compassion is always associated with feeling compassion and showing mercy. The two concepts are inseparable. If you just feel compassion without showing mercy, then you really have not experienced biblical compassion.

Biblical compassion always has a resulting action. Jesus felt compassion for the multitudes and then showed mercy. There were resulting actions that sprang from His feeling compassion. But what did Jesus see?

He saw that the crowds were "distressed and dispirited." Those words describe the spiritual and physical condition of the people. Both of these words describe people who have been mishandled by the leadership and are helpless, "like sheep without a shepherd" (Matthew 9:36).

Jesus, seeing the people's condition, responds in a number of ways.

Realizing that the harvest is plentiful and that the workers are few, He first calls His disciples to prayer.

Pause here for just a second. Do you see people in the same way that Jesus sees people? When was the last time you wept for your city or for your neighborhood in the same way that Jesus wept when He entered the city of Jerusalem (Luke 19:41)? When was the last time you prayed for your city or neighborhood?

As I drive to Dallas Theological Seminary every morning, I have the opportunity to go over a small overpass. As I reach the top of this little overpass, on a clear day I am afforded the first glance of the skyline of the city of Dallas. That is my reminder to pray for the people of Dallas. I ask God to give me His heart for this city.

Jesus' encouragement to His disciples was to "beseech the Lord of the harvest to send out workers into His harvest" (Matthew 9:38). We are to pray for the workers to reach the people. But Jesus does not stop there. Jesus summons His twelve disciples (Matthew 10:1) and sends them out (Matthew 10:5)! There is a need for our involvement in the process. It is not just seeing the need and feeling compassion. Just feeling compassion is not biblical compassion at all. Biblical compassion also has a resulting action attached. In this case, the disciples were sent out.

Do you see people in the same way that Jesus sees people? If we are becoming more and more conformed to the image of Christ, then what does that look like? One of the characteristics is that we will have a compassion for the lost.

A PASSION FOR RECONCILIATION

Third, the Father has a passion for reconciliation. As Paul explained, "Now all these things are from God, who reconciled us to Himself through Christ and gave us the ministry of reconciliation, namely, that God was in Christ reconciling the world to Himself, not counting their trespasses against them, and He has committed to us the word of reconciliation" (2 Corinthians 5:18–19).

Notice a couple of things about these verses. First, notice how many times variations of the word *reconciled* is used. Second, notice that Paul emphasizes that we have been given the "ministry of reconciliation" and entrusted with the "word of reconciliation." Even though God reconciled the world to Himself, He has committed to us the message of what He has done.

But then in verses 20 and 21, we see God's passion for this world to be spread. "Therefore, we are ambassadors for Christ, as though God were making an appeal through us; we beg you on behalf of Christ, be reconciled to God. He made Him who knew no sin to be sin on our behalf, that we might become the righteousness of God in Him." Notice the phrase, "as though God were making an appeal through us; we beg you on behalf of Christ, be reconciled to God." We beg you! You can almost feel the passion that God has, as He desires for the world to be reconciled to Him through Christ.

The amazing thing is, we have been entrusted with that message. God is entreating through us.

IN TUNE WITH THE FATHER

Why should we go across the street? Because doing so reflects the Father's heart. What does the Father's heart look like? There are many attributes, but He has a concern for the world, a compassion for the lost, and a passion for reconciliation.

There are many characteristics of biblical evangelism, but the essence of evangelism comes down to being in tune with the Father and the Father's heart. When you think about biblical evangelism, you recognize that it is centered in the person and work of Jesus Christ. It is empowered by the Holy Spirit. It is conducted in an atmosphere of prayer. And it is proclaimed through a variety of strategies. However, past all of these characteristics, we must examine our motives and see if our heart is in tune with the Father's heart. You can have all of the slickest tools, yet if it is conducted from the wrong motives, then it becomes nothing but wood, hay, and stubble.[4]

If we try to just plug away in evangelism, we begin to engage in evangelism in the flesh and not in the Spirit. Evangelism becomes a burden rather than a blessing. We have the mandate in Scripture to "go and make disciples." However, if you are just plugging away in your own power, then you are headed down a very rough road.

Here is the question: Is your heart in tune with the Father's heart? If your heart is in tune with the Father's heart, then what does that look like? You should have at least some of that same concern, compassion, and passion to reach the lost.

As a result of some further discussions, that church right across the street from the university began to take a few steps to show some interest in those students. Now there is a thriving university ministry with a staff person and evening service dedicated to reach the campus for Jesus Christ.

What about you? Do you have the picture of the Father that says, "I will just live my life and maybe someone will ask me about the Savior"? Or is your heart in tune with the Father's heart? If it is, you will have that same desire that He has to reach out to a lost world.

WHAT DID
YOU SAY?

EVANGELISM PRINCIPLE 3: *Make the Gospel clear.*

THERE WAS A PASTOR in town who was a really super guy. Very personable and friendly, he also was heavily involved in community service. He helped to establish a local rescue mission downtown, which ministered to those who were homeless and hungry. The community voucher system was a result of his efforts. He also had a major role in finding the funds for the women's shelter in town. He had played a part in the counseling center that we all took advantage of, and also coordinated the hospital and jail ministries.

If there was a community service available, most likely this pastor was involved somewhere. It appeared that he was everywhere.

One morning I met him at a breakfast and thanked him for his service. "I really appreciate the amount of time you take to lead some of these very influential types of ministries," I said. "I appreciate your work in establishing all of the ministries that are available, especially the women's shelter and the ministry to the homeless and to those who are hungry. The things that you do in this community are noticed. I appreciate your hard work. Thank you."

He stopped, looked at me, and said, "Well, that's the Gospel."

Suddenly, it became very clear to me why he was spending an enormous amount of time in community activities. Social outreach for that pastor, especially to the poor, the downtrodden, and to the suffering, was, in his mind, the Gospel.

That raises an interesting question. What is the Gospel? Is maintaining the soup kitchen downtown the Gospel? Some would say that it is. Or is the Gospel visiting the sick and feeding the hungry? After all, Matthew 25:35–36 reads, "For I was hungry, and you gave Me something to eat; I was thirsty, and you gave Me something to drink; I was a stranger, and you invited Me in; naked, and you clothed Me; I was sick, and you visited Me; I was in prison, and you came to Me." Or what about James 1:27, which says, "Pure and undefiled religion in the sight of our God and Father is this: to visit orphans and widows in their distress, and to keep oneself unstained by the world." Is that the Gospel?

My pastor friend would say, "Yes, that's the Gospel." That's the reason that he was so involved in community service.

What would you say? Is community service the Gospel . . . or part of the Gospel, demonstrating the Gospel in action? Is community service a result of the Gospel? Where does all that fit in?

A DEFINITION OF THE GOSPEL

Some of the confusion that exists may be attributed to a faulty definition of the Gospel. The Gospel can be multifaceted and confusing to people.

Various definitions of the Gospel have been offered. And just as we saw with the definition of evangelism, different definitions of the Gospel can also make the conversation very confusing. What is the Gospel, and how do we communicate it?

The word *Gospel* means "good news."[1] The Gospel is news and not an action. Various gospels have been identified as people spread the good news concerning a number of different topics. After all, you can have "good news" about a number of things. People have identified the gospel of peace (Ephesians 6:15) and the gospel of the kingdom (Matthew 24:14). These observations add another dimension not just to the word *gospel* but to the confusion of what exactly we are supposed to be proclaiming while doing the work of evangelism.

We are particularly interested in the gospel of salvation. The gospel of salvation is the "power of God" (Romans 1:16). But even the gospel of salvation can be confused in its communication. Charles Ryrie in his book *So Great Salvation* makes an interesting observation regarding the misstating of the Gospel:

> Observe this random sampling of expressions of the Gospel taken from tracts, sermons, books, and radio and TV messages. I list them without documentation since the point is not who said these but what was said, and to illustrate how varied and confusing these statements are. If we gave even half of them to an unsaved person, which and what would he be expected to believe?
>
> Here they are:
>
> 1. Repent, believe, confess your sin to God, and confess Him before men and you will be saved.
> 2. The clearest statement of the Gospel in the New Testament is found in Luke 9:23: "If any man wishes to come after Me, let him deny himself, and take up his cross daily, and follow Me."
> 3. Perhaps the most comprehensive invitation to salvation in the epistles comes in James 4:7–10: "Submit therefore to God. Resist the devil and he will flee from you. Draw near to God and He will draw near to you. Cleanse your hands, you sinners; and purify your hearts, you double-minded. Be miserable and mourn and weep; let your laughter be turned into mourning, and your joy to gloom. Humble yourselves in the presence of the Lord, and He will exalt you."
> 4. May the Lord reveal to the sinners that the only way for them to be saved from their sins is to repent with a godly sorrow in their heart to the Lord.

5. Utter the prayer of the prodigal son—ask Jesus to be your Lord and Master.
6. Come forward and follow Christ in baptism.
7. Place your hand in the nail-scarred hands of Jesus.[2]

Ryrie continues with nine other statements of the Gospel, concluding with numbers fourteen through sixteen:

14. No one can receive Christ as his Savior while he rejects Him as his Lord.
15. Give your heart to Christ.
16. Ask Jesus to come into your heart.[3]

Once again, we are interested in the good news about Jesus Christ. The Good News is that Christ has provided for salvation. Jesus Christ and what He has done for us is the Good News. This is the Gospel that we are commanded to preach. It is also the Gospel that is emphasized by Paul in his letters. Ryrie clarifies,

Paul gives us the precise definition of the Gospel we preach today in 1 Corinthians 15:3–8. The Gospel is the good news about the death and resurrection of Christ. He died and He lives—this is the content of the Gospel. . . . This same twofold content of the good news appears again in Romans 4:25: He "was delivered up . . . and was raised." Everyone who believes in that good news is saved, for that truth, and that alone, is the Gospel of the grace of God (1 Corinthians 15:2).[4]

The essence of the Good News centers on the person and work of Jesus Christ. Jesus Christ has paid the price for our sins. In theological terms we would say that He is the propitiation for our sins. He has satisfied God's justice by dying on the cross in our place. But why all this confusion regarding the Gospel? Ryrie goes on to say,

Some of the confusion regarding the meaning of the Gospel today may arise from failing to clarify the issue involved. The issue is, How can my sins be forgiven? What is it that bars me from heaven? What is it that prevents my having eternal life? The answer is sin. The second issue is, How can my sins be forgiven? I need some way to resolve that problem. And God declares that the death of His Son provides forgiveness of my sin.

"Christ died for our sins"—that's as plain as it could possibly be. Sinners need a Savior.[5]

ESSENTIALS IN COMMUNICATING THE GOSPEL: 1. SIN

The message of the Gospel has to do with three things. I look at the message that I am to proclaim as a hamburger that I am preparing to present to someone who is starving. The three topics correspond to a top bun, the meat in the middle of the sandwich—which is the essence of the Good News—and a bottom bun. All three make a complete and satisfying meal. The three topics are in order: sin, substitutionary atonement, and faith. Let's look at each one in order.

The first topic, the top bun in our sandwich, is sin. As Ryrie pointed out, sin is the main problem. As it says in 1 Corinthians 15:3, "Christ died for our sins." Sin is what bars us from heaven. "All of us like sheep have gone astray, each of us has turned to his own way; but the Lord has caused the iniquity of us all to fall on Him" (Isaiah 53:6). We need some way to deal with sin. But what exactly is sin? And how can we communicate the concept?

> Sin is anything contrary to
> the character and nature of God.

The word *sin* has about a dozen Greek words in the New Testament that describe the concept. The most frequent word that is used is *harmartia;* the root meaning is "missing the mark."[6] If we utilize all of the ways that sin is described in the New Testament, it may be defined as "missing the mark, badness, rebellion, iniquity, going astray, wickedness, wandering, ungodliness, crime, lawlessness, transgression, ignorance, and a falling away."[7]

Indeed, sin is anything contrary to the character and the nature of God. "Sin is that which proves unlike the character of God."[8] It is "missing the mark of God's standard of perfection and rebelling against Him."[9]

The chief characteristic is that all sin is ultimately directed against God. David recognized that clearly as he cried out to God, "Against You, You only, I have sinned and done what is evil in Your sight, so that You are justified when You speak and blameless when You judge" (Psalm 51:4). There are several aspects of sin that the Bible speaks about which point out our total depravity and need for a Savior.

There is inherited sin, imputed sin, and personal sin. "Inherited sin is that sinful state into which all people are born."[10] Inherited sin (Ephesians 2:3) is transmitted from generation to generation through our parents. Imputed sin (Romans 5:12) means "all sinned when Adam sinned."[11] It is the sin nature that is passed directly from Adam to me. "Humanity joined all of us to Adam and to Adam's sin. We all share in Adam's sin and Adam's guilt. We are all guilty and in need of a remedy for our sin."[12] We are guilty because Adam was guilty. A good illustration of imputed sin is when one football player jumps offsides; the whole team receives the penalty. One player makes a mistake on the field, but the entire team is penalized. When Adam sinned, we all sinned.

However, there are also personal sins that really bring home the reality of sin in our lives. Because of our nature, we all commit sins. There are sins of commission (things that we do) and sins of omission (things that we don't do when we should), but both make evident the pervasiveness of sin in our life.

Either way, "The wages of sin is death" (Romans 6:23). What is owed as a result of our sin is death. Because of our sin, we owe spiritual and physical separation from God.

Sin is universal. Sin is the problem. Sin is what keeps me from having a relationship with God. It is what bars me from heaven. Isaiah 59:2 reads, "But your iniquities have made a separation between you and your God, and your sins have hidden His face from you so that He does not hear." I need some way to deal with that problem.

ESSENTIALS IN COMMUNICATING THE GOSPEL: 2. SUBSTITUTIONARY ATONEMENT

The second part of the message, the meat of the sandwich, is the essence of the Good News. The Good News is Christ died for my sins and arose from the dead (1 Corinthians 15:1–8). Jesus died in my place. He died as my substitute. Because of my sin I deserve death, but Jesus took my penalty upon Himself and died for me. The Good News is the substitutionary atonement of Jesus Christ. The root meaning of the word *atonement* from the Old Testament is "to cover"; however, it is used to mean not only cover our sins, but also take our sins away.[13] "He made Him who knew no sin to be sin on our behalf, so that we might become the righteousness of God in Him" (2 Corinthians 5:21). "But God demonstrates His own love toward us, in that while we were yet sinners, Christ died for us" (Romans 5:8).

First Corinthians 15:1–8 is a crucial passage in our understanding of the Good News. The passage breaks down into two main parts. Verses 1 and 2 describe the *character* of the Gospel. Verses 3–8 explain the *content* of the Gospel. According to verses 1–2, Paul preached the Gospel, the Corinthians received it, they stood in it, and they were saved by it. But what is this Gospel?

The content of the Gospel is explained in verses 3–5. Paul talks about the death and resurrection of Christ. "For I delivered to you as of first importance what I also received, that Christ died for our sins according to the Scriptures, and that He was buried, and that He was raised on the third day according to the Scriptures, and that He appeared to Cephas, then to the twelve."

The Gospel ... is: Christ died
for my sins and arose from the dead.

Notice from this passage that there are two main parts: (1) Christ died for our sins, and (2) He arose from the dead. Notice now that Paul supplies biblical evidence and also empirical evidence for each statement. The statement "Christ died for our sins" is followed by the biblical evidence, "according to the Scriptures." And following the biblical evidence, Paul supplies the empirical evidence, "He was buried."

"He [also] was raised on the third day." Again, Paul supplies both biblical evidence, "according to the Scriptures," and empirical evidence, "He appeared."

With both biblical and empirical evidence, Paul declares the Good News. The Gospel, the Good News, is: Christ died for my sins and arose from the dead. That message and that message alone is the good news about Jesus Christ. That is the meat of the sandwich.

I would like to highlight one aspect of that message here by way of parenthesis. In a study I did several years ago, I compared and contrasted the apostles' preaching of the Gospel in the book of Acts with current evangelistic presentations.[14] What I found was that in presentations we are very careful to present Christ's death for our sin, yet we leave out any mention of the Resurrection! We have a tendency to leave Christ in the grave. Nothing has changed since that study was done. We still have that tendency today.

However, in the book of Acts, it was the Resurrection that caused a stir among the listeners! In fact, when Paul was speaking in Athens, "when they heard of the resurrection of the dead, some began to sneer" (Acts 17:32). The Resurrection caused a commotion. Other examples include Peter's presentation of the Gospel to the nation of Israel in Acts 2:24, 31–32; or Peter's sermon to the rulers and elders in Jerusalem in Acts 4:10. Everywhere that the apostles were preaching, they were preaching Christ's resurrection as core to what had happened.

The practicality of this is enormous! As we present the Gospel today, without much mention of the Resurrection some of the emphasis is lost, and the presentation can almost come across as wimpy. We have almost come to the place where we are apologizing for bringing the topic up. Christianity without the Resurrection is like baseball without a bat—it doesn't have any clout!

As the apostles preached the Gospel, the emphasis on the Resurrection came through loud and clear. Christ died for your sins *and arose from the dead* as proof that His sacrifice was acceptable to God! Romans 4:25 states, "He . . . was delivered over because of our transgressions, and was raised because of our justification." Sin, death, and the devil have been conquered. He is alive! And He is coming back. And when He comes back He is coming back as judge. Now that is good news!

The Good News is that Christ died for our sins and arose from the dead. Finally, Paul notes that this Gospel is what he and others preached and the Corinthians had believed. He says, "Whether then it was I or they, so we preach and so you believed" (1 Corinthians 15:11). This is the genuine item! Both emphasize the substitutionary atonement of Jesus Christ that was made on our behalf. Sin and substitutionary atonement form the first two parts of our presentation.

ESSENTIALS IN COMMUNICATING
THE GOSPEL: 3. FAITH

The third part to our presentation, the bottom bun of our sandwich, is faith. Faith and trust in Jesus Christ and His substitutionary atonement is the only way to be reconciled to God. Paul said, "So we preach and so you believed" (1 Corinthians 15:11). Paul preached it, and the Corinthians believed it. Faith not only involves the knowledge of the facts and intellectual assent to those facts, but the appropriation of the facts to oneself. The word *faith* comes from the root word for trust and believe.[15]

Faith involves transferring your trust from whatever you are currently trusting in to make yourself right with God (e.g., your good works, your church membership) to what Christ has already accomplished on the Cross on your behalf.

There is no way that you can earn your way to heaven. There is no way that you can make yourself any more acceptable to God. Trusting in Christ and Christ alone is the only way to be reconciled to a holy God.

From the beginning of time, trusting in the sacrifice was the only way to be reconciled to a holy God. The substitutionary atonement has its roots in the very beginning of human history. God provided the skins of animals as clothing for Adam and Eve in Genesis 3:21. He allowed the blood of an unblemished lamb to protect the nation during the Passover in Exodus 12. The sacrificial system in Leviticus 1–7 and the Day of Atonement in Leviticus 16 called for the deaths of a bull and a ram as God's provision for sin. Isaiah made reference to the suffering servant who would die as a substitute for the sins of the world (Isaiah 52:14–53:12).

When Jesus appeared, John the Baptist declared Him as "the Lamb of God who takes away the sins of the world" (John 1:29). Jesus gave His life as a substitutionary atonement for our sins. He died in our place (2 Corinthians 5:21). Hebrews 10:12 says that He "offered one sacrifice for sins for all time."

From the beginning, then, the issue has been to deal with sin by grace through faith in the provision of a subsitutionary atonement. As a gift of grace, God provided His Son as a substitutionary atonement for sin. Through faith we accept the gift.

All that we need to do is believe. But what is faith? Is faith some blind leap off a cliff? Faith is only as effective as its object. To truly have faith and believe in the biblical sense, you must have total confidence and trust in something or someone; otherwise you merely have faith in faith. The object of our faith is Jesus Christ.

Faith involves three basic elements: (1) the knowledge of the facts, (2) an intellectual assent to those facts, and (3) an act of volition to appropriate those facts to myself.

> Belief in [Jesus] alone
> will reconcile you to God.

The essential facts of the Gospel are that Christ died for our sins and arose from the dead (1 Corinthians 15:3–4). But faith also requires an intellectual assent to those facts. It is one thing to know the facts, but it is quite another to agree with them and accept them as being true. Accepting something as true does not mean that there is no investigation of the facts. Faith does not mean believing when there is no evidence. Faith believes the facts and the evidence as true.

Finally, biblical faith includes an act of volition to appropriate those facts to oneself. The special part of faith is trusting Jesus Christ as the only way of salvation, believing that His death paid for your sins and that such trust in Him and Him alone will reconcile you to God, bringing forgiveness of your sins and eternal life.

The object of our faith is Jesus Christ. The issue is whether we trust in Him and what He did as the only acceptable sacrifice for our sins. Jesus said, "He who believes in the Son has eternal life" (John 3:36). Paul declared, "Believe in the Lord Jesus, and you will be saved" (Acts 16:31).

The Bible always teaches that salvation is by grace through faith (Ephesians 2:8–9). Faith in itself does not save anyone; it is faith in Jesus Christ that saves. Let's try to put this all together in an illustration.

I can have faith in a lot of things. I can have faith that an airplane can fly. In fact, I exhibit a lot of faith when I travel across the country in an airplane. I never check out whether the pilot has a pilot's license. I never check out the airworthiness papers to see whether the aircraft has all of its required inspections up-to-date. I merely trust that those things are true. I believe that an airplane can fly. I can stand inside the terminal and have that intellectual assent in the airline's ability to get me from point A to point B, but it is not until I crawl onto that airplane and strap myself in that I "believe" in the biblical sense of the word. I have now committed my life to that belief.

Let's take my airplane illustration a bit further. Let us say that while I am in the air the plane has an emergency that requires the pilot to ditch the aircraft in the ocean. Some passengers are killed on impact. The airplane is sinking; however, there are emergency life vests under all the seats, plus the escape slides double as rafts. Among the survivors, one man is unaware that rafts are available. (He was not listening to the safety briefing at the beginning of the flight and it is dark inside the airplane.) He does not make it to the escape hatch because he doesn't have the knowledge; so he is lost. Another man knows about the life vests and the rafts, yet he is so broken up about losing his wife in the crash that he chooses to remain in the airplane and go down with his wife. He has knowledge and even believes that the rafts can save him, yet he makes a choice to not get into the raft. He has knowledge of the facts, and even has an intellectual assent to the facts, yet he will be lost.

The rest of the people have the knowledge, they believe the flight attendants when they say that the raft will save their lives, and they get into the raft. It is not their faith that shall save them; it is the raft that shall save them. The raft through faith will save them.[16]

Our faith is in Jesus Christ, who He is and what He has done on our behalf. Jesus Christ died for our sins and arose from the dead. Trusting in Him and Him alone is the only way to be saved.

MAKING IT CLEAR: THE CRUCIFIED
AND RESURRECTED CHRIST

Let's return to my friend who was involved in all types of activities in the community. He was convinced that his social activity was the Gospel. Is the local soup kitchen the Gospel? No, it is a bridge into a person's life to be able to present the Gospel. It is a necessary bridge if the person is starving to death, but the Gospel is *Christ died for my sins and arose from the dead.* Giving a starving man a sandwich or some soup will provide a way into his life to then be able to present the Good News.

My friend had the Gospel confused. He had confused the means by which to enter into a person's life to be able to share the Good News with the Good News itself. As we talked further at that breakfast, I was able to make the distinction clear. Which brings me to Cecil's principles of evangelism number three: *Make the Gospel clear.*

The communication of the Gospel has three main ingredients: sin, substitutionary atonement, and faith. The meat of the sandwich, the essence of the Good News, is that Christ died for our sins and arose from the dead. Keep the main thing the main thing. Make it clear.

SEVEN:
SPRINGING FROM THE INSIDE OUT

EVANGELISM PRINCIPLE 4: *Evangelism is more spiritual than methodological.*

IMAGINE YOURSELF LIVING in upstate New York; the year is 1848. For years you have lived within the rumbling sound of 200,000 cubic feet of water per second pouring over the Niagara Falls. Then on March 29 you are startled by the sound of silence.

On March 29, 1848, the Niagara Falls stopped.

People were in a quandary. Again, imagine you are there. Some of your neighbors are thinking the world is coming to an end. Others hear about friends exploring the riverbed for the first time, finding relics from the war of 1812. What are you thinking?

It must have been a wild time. Today the prevailing theory is that icebergs from Lake Erie had broken up and jammed the mouth of the Niagara some miles upstream, causing the falls to come to a trickle. For some hours the falls stopped, until the force behind the icebergs caused them to shift and the falls returned to normal.

The falls were created to flow freely. They were created to flow without any obstructions or barriers.

Let me ask you a question. Out of the total flow of life that God wants to pass through you, how much actually makes it through? Or how much is being blocked by some obstruction? Jesus said that He came "that they may have life, and have it abundantly" (John 10:10). How much of that abundant life are you actually experiencing? How much of that life is being jammed up by some obstruction in your life?

When I go into my backyard and turn on the water faucet, I have water flowing out of the garden hose at the other end. I can hinder that flow by merely putting a kink in the hose. You can have a water hose flowing very freely with a lot of power, but when you kink the hose, the flow becomes a trickle; it can even stop completely.

We have been created in such a way that we will never experience the fullness of what God might have for us until we are able to allow the Holy Spirit to flow freely through us. Out of the total flow of life that God wants to pass through us, much may be stopped due to some kink in the system. That kink in the system is some type of sin in one's life.

For you, it may be in the form of a habitual sin that has drawn your focus somewhere other than Jesus Christ. It could be pride. It could be fear of what people may think of you. Most of the time in evangelism we are afraid that people might not like us, and we become more concerned with what people think than what God thinks.

The problem is, when we feel the obstruction, when we come to grips with the kinks in our life, we try to solve the problem in the flesh. When we thirst for that abundance of life, we often search for that life in all the wrong places. People might turn to a set of rules or regulations to start on that path of fullness and life. Or people may turn to the latest book or seminar on the subject, thinking that life is found there.

SATISFYING OUR THIRST:
A FEAST TO REMEMBER

How can we satisfy our thirstiness? A passage that points to the answers (and has impacted me greatly) is John 7:37–39.[1]

A little background to this passage might be helpful to its understanding. The context of this passage is the Feast of Booths, also known as the Feast of Tabernacles (Leviticus 23:33–43). The Feast of Booths happened around October. It was one of the three great feasts that the nation would celebrate. In fact, Josephus, the Roman historian, referred to the Feast of Booths as the holiest and the greatest of the feasts.

It was also called the feast of ingatherings, a time of thanksgiving for the harvest. It was a happy time. Devout Jews lived outdoors in booths made of tree branches for seven days as a reminder of God's provision in the desert during the wilderness wanderings. There were a lot of festive rituals that were celebrated during the feast. There were two practices that were not mentioned in Scripture but were included in the oral tradition passed on from Moses. One was the "special commandment of the willow," and the other was the water libation.[2]

Each morning there was a solemn procession from the temple mount to the pool of Siloam for a pitcher of water. A priest would fill a gold pitcher with water as the people sang together from Isaiah 12:3, "Therefore you will joyously draw water from the springs of salvation." The procession would return to the temple mount with trumpets blasting and great fanfare; there the priest would pour the water into a silver basin by the altar of burnt offering each day for the first seven days.

As historian Chaim Richman has noted, "The actual participants in the celebrations were not the common folk, but the greatest scholars and the most pious men of the generation—the heads of the Sanhedrin, the sages, the academy heads and the elders. In the presence of all those assembled in the Holy Temple, these exceedingly righteous men would dance, sing and rejoice."[3]

The ritual was designed to look in three directions. It looked back and reminded the people of how God had provided water from the rock during the wilderness wanderings (Numbers 20:8–11). It looked at the present and praised God for the provision of the harvest and most likely acted as a prayer for the coming year (Psalm 118:25). But the ritual also looked toward the future and spoke prophetically of the coming days of the Messiah when God's blessing would be poured out on the nation (Zechariah 14:8, 16–19).

This ritual had taken place for six days by the time Jesus spoke to the people in the John 7 passage. "Now on the last day, the great day of the feast, Jesus stood and cried out, saying, 'If anyone is thirsty, let him come to Me and drink'" (v. 37).

Six times the procession to the pool of Siloam had taken place. This was the last day.[4] It was early in the morning after a night of worship. They had all gathered waiting for the sun to come up.

What I envision possibly happening, even though Scripture doesn't tell us, is that the priest had returned to the temple mount with the pitcher of water. He climbed the long ramp to the top of the altar. Once at the top, he would turn to where the libations were poured. Two silver cups were on top of the altar, one filled with wine, the other awaiting the libation.[5]

The priest began to slowly pour the water out of the pitcher. It is at this moment that Jesus stood in the midst of the crowd and cried out, "If anyone is thirsty, let him come to Me and drink." What was He saying? In effect, Jesus was declaring, "You have just tasted the best that religion and ritualism has to offer. This is it! This is as good as it gets! If you are still thirsty, and if you don't find all of this ritual satisfying, then come to Me and drink."

Maybe the disciples crawled under their mats at this moment. "Oh no, here He goes again. Every time we take Him into a public arena He causes a disturbance!" But Jesus knew that there were many who felt empty. Jesus knew that there were those who were just going through the motions, hoping to find life and not finding satisfaction. Jesus was offering them abundant life.

But the parallel thought is powerful. Are you trying to find life in places other than Jesus Christ? Are you thirsty? Are you searching for that abundance in life? If you are still thirsty in your spiritual walk with Christ—if you are still thirsty in evangelism, still thirsty in your life itself—come to Jesus and drink. Notice a few important items in this statement that Jesus makes about coming to the right source.

SATISFYING OUR THIRST: THE RIGHT SOURCE

First, Jesus says that you need to go to the right source. Jesus says that you need to come *to Him* to drink.

It is interesting that when I find myself thirsty in my spiritual life, I am tempted to go to everywhere *except* Jesus to find satisfaction. One of the temptations that we have when we feel inadequate in evangelism is to run to the latest book in evangelism, or run to the latest seminar in evangelism to try to quench our thirst, rather than going to the source of Jesus Christ.

But Jesus says that you need to come to the right source. Jesus quenches our thirst personally, not by proxy. It is easy to get caught up with all of the other trappings of life and not experience the fullness of Jesus Christ Himself.

Many years ago I had an old pastor say to me, "Untended fires soon die and become just a pile of ashes."[6] I like this image. It is an appropriate image that describes my time with the Lord. We all need to spend time tending the fire within; it is the basis for everything else we do. Jesus calls us first to a relationship with Him (Mark 3:14). But tending that fire is your responsibility (James 4:8; 1 Timothy 4:7). We need to make time to properly tend to that relationship with Jesus Christ.

A good fire keeps you warm, and it keeps others warm as well. As long as that fire is tended within you it will satisfy your needs and also warm others. The basic kindling needed for tending that fire includes Bible study and prayer. The not-so-obvious kindling needed to properly tend that inner fire are activities like silence, solitude, and Scripture memory. All contribute to a properly tended fire.

When you begin to experience the emptiness and become thirsty for the abundance of life, is Jesus Christ the first source that you turn to? Is He where you run when you feel the thirst?

COMING TO THE SOURCE AGAIN AND AGAIN

Second, Jesus says that you need to *keep coming* to the source. The tense of the verb here is present imperative, which is a continuous action command. "Keep coming. Keep drinking from the source!" Jesus was inviting everyone to continue to come and continue to drink from the proper source.

One of the greatest struggles we all have is trying to keep our daily time with the Lord consistent. We begin to rationalize our behavior with statements like "I am too busy" or "I have too many things on my plate right now." I realize that at the very root of my problem is that I would rather drink from the broken cistern of man's approval, thinking that abundant life is found there, rather than from the spring of living water that Jesus offers.

Life is not found in keeping a set of rules and regulations. Life is not found in writing a book. Life is not found in doing more things. Life is found in Jesus Christ. We cannot be rivers of living water to others if an obstruction at the source is blocking the flow of the Holy Spirit through us.

In the book of Revelation, Jesus speaks to the church at Ephesus. He condemns the church for leaving their first love (Revelation 2:4). Maybe you have left your first love. We are hard-pressed to have impact in a lost world without the power that flows from the source of Jesus Christ.

Where do we find satisfaction and life? We find it by first going to the right source and continuing to come to the right source.

There are some results that are described in John 7:38–39. (The cause is in verse 37, the effect in verses 38–39.) Jesus says, "He who believes in Me, as the Scripture said, 'From his innermost being will flow rivers of living water.' But this He spoke of the Spirit, whom those who believed in Him were to receive; for the Spirit was not yet given, because Jesus was not yet glorified" (John 7:38–39).

I understand verse 37, but what in the world are verses 38 and 39 talking about? Jesus is talking about streams of living water flowing from my innermost being.

We know from John 4 that the living water is Jesus Himself. In John 4:10–26, Jesus says that He is the living water. He is the One who provides life and gives eternal life. But here in John 7, Jesus links that living water with the flow of the Holy Spirit in me. Whoever believes becomes a source of that living water for others. Whoever believes becomes a channel for that living water to flow to a world that is thirsty.

In other words, the message of Christ flows through the believer by the power of the Holy Spirit to a lost world . . . unless there is a kink in the system.

HOW TO HAVE THAT LIVING WATER FLOW

As we dwell at the source of Jesus Christ, the living water will flow. Notice that there are four characteristics that describe this process in the verses that follow. There are four phrases and words that give us insight into this process of allowing this living water to flow through us to a lost world.

First, the flow of living water is available to "whoever believes." Notice that Jesus' offer is all-inclusive. It is open to everyone—"whoever believes." In other words, becoming a source of living water to a lost world is not just for those who are more gifted in evangelism. It is not just for those who have the "bent" for evangelism; it is for everyone who believes.

In our Christian culture we tend to believe that evangelism is only for the gifted. I often hear phrases like, "I just do not have the ability to be able to be involved in evangelism." However, that mind-set contradicts what the passage says. The passage tells me that anyone who believes has the ability to reproduce in Christ.

Evangelism is very similar to giving. We may not all have the gift of giving, but we are all called to participate in giving and are able to experience some of the blessings associated with the privilege of giving. In similar fashion, we might not all have the gift of evangelism; however, we are all called to be able to participate in evangelism and experience some of the blessings that are associated with evangelism.

Second, there is an inexhaustible source of living water available. Jesus says that "streams" of living water will flow from the believer. The word could really be translated as "floods," or "torrents." There will be a Niagara Falls experience of water that will flow through the believer.

God is not calling us to be involved in anything that He has not given us the ability to pull off. He has the ability and the availability to be able to accomplish the task. He is just asking us to allow Him to work.

> Your Father in heaven
> has deep pockets.

This is of great encouragement to me. Often in evangelism I feel inadequate to be a worthy ambassador for Christ. I am tempted to say, as Moses said, "Send my brother instead." However, God has provided us an abundant resource in Jesus Christ if we will only allow ourselves to rest in that resource.

Periodically I invite the family out to dinner. When we go out to eat at a restaurant, I always seem to be the one who is left with the bill. At the end of the meal, everyone looks to me to pay what is owed. There is never a thought that Dad will not be able to pay the bill. It is expected that Dad will pay, because after all, I have invited them out. There is never a thought that the resources would not be available to satisfy the debt that has accrued. In fact, usually just the opposite is true. The thought usually is, "Dad has deep pockets, so let's eat up!"

Your Father in heaven has deep pockets. He has made the resources available to pull off what He has called us to do.

Third, the living water is alive! Jesus says that streams of *"living"* water will flow from the innermost being. Living water is the best source of the water.

In ancient Israel, three sources of water existed. There was well water. People would dig down to the water table and then lift water in buckets from the well. Well water was not a bad source of water. Jacob's well is an example in Scripture of well water. In fact, Jacob's well was where the woman at the well (John 4:12) drew water as Jesus engaged her in dialogue.

Another source of water was cistern water. Cistern water was the worst source of water. People would dig trenches in the dirt to collect the rainwater runoff. The trenches would funnel the rainwater into an underground cistern, which was dug out of the ground and plastered to make a great underground pot.

Such water had a lot of dirt collected in the bottom. The water was stagnant. This was the least desirable source of water.

But there was a third source of water in Israel: living water. Living water was the water that came from the springs. The cool spring waters came from the snow runoff on Mount Hermon. A great example of living water is the Banias Waterfall close to Caesarea Philippi in Galilee. The waterfall appears to be coming out of the rock; however, it is the runoff from Mount Hermon that has soaked through the porous limestone in the area as it flows toward the Jordan River.

This water is alive with oxygen. It is cool, flowing, and refreshing. It is the best source of water.

Qumran, a community of Essenes who lived in the desert region by the Dead Sea, is where the Dead Sea Scrolls were found. The community had only one source of water, and that was cistern water. Today visitors to the Qumran community can view many underground cisterns. I always like to stop by one particular cistern on the way back to the hospitality house at Qumran. This cistern is relatively large, but the distinguishing characteristic about this cistern is that there is a large two-inch crack that runs from the top to the bottom.

When I stop at this site, I love to read a portion from Jeremiah. "My people have committed two sins: They have forsaken me, the spring of living water, and have dug their own cisterns, broken cisterns that cannot hold water" (Jeremiah 2:13 NIV).

That is exactly what we have done! We would rather drink from our manmade cisterns, thinking that life is found there, than from the living water that Jesus has provided. We would rather drink from some stagnant puddle of mud than from the running, cool, clear, refreshing Rocky Mountain springwater. Which would you rather choose?

Jesus says that this flow of water is available for everyone who believes. It is in abundance, and it is alive!

> [Through] the Holy Spirit, sharing the good news
> about Jesus Christ becomes a passion.

Fourth, the living water will flow from our innermost being. Jesus says that the water "will" flow. It is an absolute. When the Holy Spirit lives within you there is a divine restlessness that is never satisfied until it is given full freedom of expression by flowing forth to a lost world.

If you know Jesus Christ, you already have a heart for evangelism. You do not need to try to manufacture a heart for evangelism. Because of the indwelling ministry of the Holy Spirit, sharing Jesus Christ with a lost world is already a part of your life! At the deepest part of our being, because of the ministry of the Holy Spirit, sharing the good news about Jesus Christ becomes a passion and not merely a doctrinal belief.

This also is a great encouragement to me. I do not need to try to manufacture evangelism in the flesh. I do not need to try to work myself up to do evangelism. All I need to do is appropriate what God has already placed within. I do not need to conjure up evangelism in my life but allow the Holy Spirit to work through my life. This moves evangelism off of my "to do" list and allows me to just love people!

There is nothing magical or mystical about this. Galatians 5:25 reads, "If we live by the Spirit, let us also walk by the Spirit." The way that you were saved is the same way in which you should walk—by grace through faith. Take it by faith. Trust the Holy Spirit to work through you.

We have been designed to experience the fullness of life. We will never experience the fullness of what God has for us until we allow Him to have full rein of our lives and allow Him to flow freely through us.

Jesus says that we need to go to the right source and that we need to allow Him to flow freely through us to a lost world. We need to allow the message of Christ to flow freely through us by the power of the Holy Spirit.

This should be the normal experience of every believer in Christ. Through the indwelling of the Holy Spirit, there should be some of that divine sense of the lost condition of the unsaved and the prompting by the Spirit to do whatever might be necessary to share with them the Good News, with the intent that they would place their trust in Christ alone for their salvation.

Are you allowing the Holy Spirit to flow freely in your life, or is there some type of blockage that is obstructing the flow?

DEVELOPING A PASSION

Maybe you have not felt the strongest tug of passion toward evangelism. I do believe that in some sense passion can be cultivated and learned. Passion follows obedience. I have a friend who is passionate about fishing. He lives to fish. Now do I think that he was born with a passion for fishing? No, his passion was learned. However, with evangelism, because of the Holy Spirit living within you there is a new heart for evangelism. A passion for evangelism already lives within because of the Holy Spirit; yet you can cultivate that passion by being obedient to His Word.

Years ago I was counseling a man who was wrestling with a particular decision in His life. Specifically the decision was whether he would step out in faith and trust God to meet his financial needs or rely on his own efforts and abilities.

As I talked with this man, it became evident that this decision had been faced before. In fact, we were able to look back at this man's life and point out three separate occasions when he had a similar choice. Each time, the man had made the choice to rely on his own efforts.

As we talked about these choices, it became evident that he knew what he should do but had chosen the way that appeared to him to be the most secure. But it had not brought happiness. He was not experiencing the abundant life.

Now he was faced with another opportunity to trust God. As I pointed out the other similar decisions that he had made in the past and the consequences as a result of his decision, he stopped. He began to literally pound on the table and cry, "All that I have ever done in my life is squelch God!"

At this moment this man was able to see a pattern in his life of opportunities missed. He was able to see the results of his decisions. God in His great grace was providing this man with another opportunity.

Maybe he had believed that he could find life on his own. He believed that he could manufacture life in his own power. He was holding onto his pride; he was holding onto worldly security. Through a number of poor decisions, he came to the place where he recognized that being obedient to God was really the only viable option.

What are you holding on to? What is obstructing the flow in your life? Where is the kink in the system? It could be pride. It could be fear that others may not like you. Some of us fear what other people might think of us. More important to consider is what our Lord thinks about us. Ask yourself, *Am I more concerned about what people think about me than where they will spend eternity?*

Only as you see yourself in Christ and are secure in Christ and allow the Holy Spirit to flow freely through you will you be able to experience the abundant life. Not until you allow those floodgates to be open wide in your life will you experience the exuberance of life in Christ.

> The main question in evangelism is,
> What's holding you back?

Lewis Sperry Chafer refers to this as the "Cleansing of the Priest."[7] At the very root of my being, I need to allow the Holy Spirit to have free rein in my life and work in conjunction with Him. Chafer writes, "Thus when the believer-priest is cleansed and in a normal relation to God, the Spirit is free to take every necessary step in the 'power of God unto salvation,' and the believer will be led into perfect co-operation with Christ in His great unfinished work of seeking the lost."[8]

God is the author of conversion. He is the only One able to lift that veil that blinds men's hearts. We can have the greatest techniques, but He is the only One who will bring about salvation. We may believe that we have the greatest tool for evangelism; however, it is only a tool that God is going to be able to use.

The question in evangelism is not how you can get better equipped or find the newest and latest method of sharing the Good News. The main question in evangelism is, What's holding you back? If you have placed your trust in Jesus Christ, because of the ministry of the Holy Spirit in your life, sharing Jesus Christ is a passion.

This brings about the fourth principle of evangelism: *Evangelism is more spiritual than it is methodological.* We will consider this more in the next chapter.

EIGHT:
BEING FAITHFUL

SUPPOSE THAT IN your church you are assigned the responsibilities for evangelism. This comes as a little bit of a surprise to you; yet you are happy to consent and give it your best effort. You begin to plan out how evangelism is going to take place in that particular environment.

Of course, you first pull out your copy of *The 7 Principles of an Evangelistic Life* to review what Cecil had to say on the subject! Then you begin to do a little research to find out what your church has done in the past. What has worked at the church? What has not worked? You also begin to check around to learn a little about the community and the type of people that you are trying to reach. What worked a few years ago might not work now.

Based upon some of your initial findings, you decide that the best way to proceed in this little church is to start a church visitation program. With that decision, you prepare for an all-day Saturday training session. You begin to pray that God would raise up twenty-five people to attend your evangelism training session.

You plan out the Saturday. You put up signs all over the church.

You make an announcement from the pulpit and even have a flyer in the bulletin to remind people of the upcoming seminar. You prepare the room. You buy the coffee and the donuts—you have to have donuts—and make sure all of the materials are available.

Saturday comes and six people show up. You are initially a little disappointed; however, you realize that these are the six people whom God has provided, so you do the best you can and proceed with the seminar. The people are excited and are looking forward to the practical application of the material. You tell them that the group will meet again on Tuesday evening at the church for the purpose of going out into the community to visit those individuals who have visited the church within the past couple of months.

Tuesday evening comes around. You have gathered the names of all of the visitors from the past few months and put them on 3x5 cards and sorted the cards according to zip codes. You divide your six volunteers into two groups of three people each and give each team one of the two packets of cards. "Visit as many individuals as you can between seven and nine o'clock. When you return there will be some refreshments and time to share with one another what has happened during your visits." Each team goes out.

At nine o'clock both teams return. You turn to one team leader and inquire what happened during their time. The team leader is ecstatic.

"Whoa! It was great!" he exclaims. "We went by one house where there was a mom, dad, and four kids. They all sat down and we were able to share the Gospel with them. And . . . they all came to place their trust in Christ! In fact, they had a swimming pool in their backyard and we were able to go into their backyard and baptize them. They will be in church on Sunday and want to invite their next-door neighbors as guests."

"That's great!" you reply. "It is good to see the Lord using you!"

You turn to the next fellow to inquire about his experience. "How did it go with you?"

The fellow drops his eyes to the floor and responds, "Well, at the first house, there was a mom and two kids. However it was bath time and didn't seem like a great time to visit. We went to the second house, but nobody was home. The third house we went to had a big gate to enter the yard. And between the gate and the house was a big dog that did not appear to be too friendly. We decided not to risk our lives with the dog, so we went to get some ice cream."

"Thanks," you reply. "Next Tuesday, let's try again."

Next Tuesday comes around. You mix up the teams and send them out in two groups of three with some new cards.

They return at nine o'clock, where you have prepared some goodies and refreshments. You turn to the first leader and ask once again how the evening went.

"Whoa!" he exclaims. "It was super!" And once again he goes into a story of the number of people who came to know Christ that evening and the impact that they had in the community over the past two hours. You acknowledge his service for the Lord and turn to the other leader.

"How did your evening go?" you ask. The other leader drops his eyes down to the floor once again and recounts the story of the number of houses where no one was home, or the people were unavailable. This week, however, they decided to go out for some pie instead of ice cream.

LOOKING FOR RESULTS

After a few weeks of watching this scenario unfold, one of the men in the group comes up to you and says, "Pastor, I have watched these two groups for the last couple of weeks. The one leader has amazing things happen. Let's be honest; I just can't do that. I will never be like that guy or be able to approach folks the way that he does. I am just not cut out for this ministry. I am going to go back to the nursery." What are you going to say to that dear brother?

The fact is, he may really belong in the nursery. Maybe that is where he needs to be. But in my mind I do not want him to go back to the nursery for the wrong reason. If he is going back to the nursery because he feels that he can't live up to some other person's reputation, then he is going back to the nursery for the wrong reason.

If, however, he really feels called to the nursery ministry and that is where he can best contribute to the ministry, then I would be the first person to encourage him in his calling. I just do not want him going back to the nursery because he is measuring his effectiveness on things that he can see.

Often in ministry, you may not be able to see the results of what you are doing. The reason you may not be able to see results is because you are dealing in the spiritual realm. You may or may not be able to see what is happening in the eternal. If you can, praise God!

GOD ASKS ONLY THAT WE BE FAITHFUL

When my wife, Patty, first went to the University of Cincinnati (U.C.), she attended a service at a local church. That church had a visitation program similar to the program that I described above. After that first Sunday, on a Tuesday evening a team of three individuals came to visit her at her dormitory. They had a time of pleasant conversation and then asked her if she knew what happens to a person after he or she dies. Patty was not quite sure but thought that the person would go to heaven.

The next question that the team posed to her was if she knew what would happen to *her* when *she* died. She responded that she thought that she would go to heaven.

The last question was the kicker. They asked Patty that if she were to die that night and go to heaven, and standing before God He were to ask her why He should let her into heaven, what would she say?[1] Patty responded that because she had been a good person, because she had done all of the right things, and because of her merits, God would let her into heaven.

The leader of the group responded, "Patty, there is no way that you deserve to go to heaven. You can't work your way to heaven. Heaven is not earned, it is not deserved; it is a free gift of God's grace for all to have."

At that moment, you could have probably pushed Patty over with a feather. She was shocked! She had never heard anything like that before.

Now, I know that the team probably communicated the entire Gospel presentation; however, Patty did not hear a word of it. Her brain had stopped at the moment that the leader said, "There is no way that you can work your way to heaven."

As they finished up, they left some material with Patty. They left with her a tract on how she could come to place her trust in Jesus Christ.

The team went back to the church. I am sure that they had a wrap-up session where each group shared what had transpired that evening. They probably got around to that group leader who recounted their visit to a young woman at U.C. He probably was excited yet frustrated to report, "We were able to share the Gospel with her, but all we got was a blank stare. She did not seem to understand." Finally, the group ended with prayer for that young lady.

What they did not know was that Patty's brain had stopped at the last question, and she really did not hear a word they said after that. That team could have been discouraged as a result of that evening. They could have even felt that maybe their evening was a waste of time. They did not see any results.

However, what they don't know is the rest of the story. As a result of that visit, Patty was haunted for the entire semester asking herself, *I do not deserve to go to heaven? . . . There is no way that I can earn my way to heaven?*

She went home after the fall semester for the Christmas break, but those questions still plagued her. When she returned to U.C. for the spring semester, she could not wait to get back to her dorm room and find the literature that the team had left more than three months earlier.

When she found the literature and read how she could place her trust in Jesus Christ, she trusted Christ. Patty came to know Christ as a result of that team's ministry. But that team will not know the rest of the story until we all get to heaven. From their perspective, nothing happened.

All God asks of us is to be faithful. Our success is not based on what we can see; it is based on just being faithful to what God has commanded us.

THE WIDGET MENTALITY

We usually try to measure success based on the wrong things. Normally, our natural tendency is to measure our effectiveness on things that we can count or see. We delight in trying to count church membership, converts, or the number of contacts we are able to accumulate. We want to be able to see how many people are now coming to the church as a result of our ministry. But, "God sees not as man sees, for man looks at the outward appearance, but the Lord looks at the heart" (1 Samuel 16:7).

We have our focus on the external things rather than on the internal things. For our dear brother in the above illustration, he was trying to compare himself to another brother. He was measuring his effectiveness by someone else's effectiveness.

This is what I refer to as the widget mentality. Typically in business we measure our output by the number of widgets that we are able to produce. We put raw materials into a big machine, and out the other side come widgets. We are able to count the widgets and therefore we are able to measure our effectiveness.

But that does not always work in the spiritual realm. You may or may not be able to see what is happening.

Suppose the church leadership calls the pastor in for an annual review. In the review the executive board challenges him about the amount of time he is spending in counseling. The pastor does not feel that the time is excessive; however, he promises to do better the following year. The next review comes around, and the time sheets reveal that the pastor is spending the same amount of time in counseling. Once again, the board gives the poor pastor a hard time and tells him to do better.

After a few years the pastor begins to realize what the root of the problem really is: The board wants to see substantial results from the counseling. They see hurting people going into the "machine"; however, they do not see spiritual giants coming out the other side. It does not mean that nothing is happening; it just means that the board can't see it.

So, the next year the pastor goes into the review with a suggestion. He says to the board, "Suppose I came in to this meeting with a time sheet that reflected that I spent two days a week in prayer. What would you say?"

We say that prayer is essential to ministry. We say that prayer is hard work; however, the rubber meets the road when we are faced with a time sheet that says that we spend two days a week in prayer. Some of the issues involved are trust and whether we have the widget mentality. If we only look for external signs, then the two days in prayer immediately become suspect. On the other hand, if we believe that we may not be able to see what happens in the spiritual realm, then the two days in prayer become honorable.

WAYS GOD MAY DRAW PEOPLE TO THE TRUTH

We are not the only tool that God chooses to use in the process of drawing people to His truth. We are only one of the tools that God is able to use to draw people to the truth. He is able to use a variety of things in a person's life to soften and incline him or her toward the Gospel.[2]

God's Word says that *creation* is one thing used to soften people toward the Gospel. In Romans 1:20 we read, "For since the creation of the world His invisible attributes, His eternal power and divine nature, have been clearly seen, being understood through what has been made, so that they are without excuse." David was moved by the majesty of creation in Psalm 8. Teenagers are moved to consider the reality of God as they sit by the campfire and see the stars above their heads. Dads are moved to consider the reality of God as they watch the birth of their first child.

Creation is not the Gospel. But it can be used by the Holy Spirit to prompt people to consider the claims of Christ.

A person's *conscience* is another means God uses to draw people to the truth. Romans 2:15 reads, "The work of the Law [is] written in their hearts, their conscience bearing witness, and their thoughts alternately accusing or else defending them." People seem to inherently know when good and bad is taking place.

Scriptures are often used by God to soften people to the Gospel. Bibles left in hotel rooms or hospital rooms are used by the Holy Spirit to address the problems that travelers or patients face. It is amazing how God's Word will not come back void. Isaiah 55:11 reads, "So will My word be which goes forth from My mouth; it will not return to Me empty." God is able to use Scripture even without an evangelist present.

The story of John Newton is a good example of God using Scripture in ways that seem unlikely to us. John Newton was born in 1725 to a Christian mother and a sea-merchant father. His mother was dedicated to his education. By the age of four John could read, and by his own admission, "She stored my memory with many valuable pieces, chapters and portions of Scripture, hymns and poems."[3] John's mother died when he was only thirteen days away from his seventh birthday. Accounts differ, but after his mother died he went to live with a non-Christian relative who mocked and persecuted John.

He joined his father's ship at age eleven, but at sixteen a press gang jumped him and forced him to sail on a British man-of-war. Eventually he escaped; however, he was captured and publicly flogged as a deserter.

He finally deserted the navy once more and ran away to Africa, "to sin his fill." He ended up sailing with a slave trader in West Africa and eventually ended up a slave to the slave trader's wife. She humiliated him, and he lived hungry for two years.

Newton ran away and was picked up by a ship on its way back to England. But he couldn't even keep that job! He broke into the ship's rum supply and in a drunken stupor fell into the sea. The only way that the ship's officers were able to save him was to harpoon him, leaving a fist-sized scar in his thigh.

By age twenty-two, Newton found himself on a small island off the coast of North Africa. The verses that his mother had planted in John's memory began to come back to him. "Weak and almost delirious, I arose from my bed and crept to a secluded part of the island; there I found a renewed liberty to pray. I made no more resolves, but cast myself before the Lord to do with me as He should please. I was enabled to hope and believe in a crucified Savior. The burden was removed from my conscience."[4]

John Newton was the man who wrote "Amazing Grace." His mother never knew, but God was able to take verses that had been hidden away in John's memory some sixteen years earlier to bring John to Himself. God is able to use a variety of tools to soften people to the Gospel.

A tragedy [or] a hospital stay may
wake up a person to ... the Lord.

The Holy Spirit is also at work in an unbeliever's life. "And He, when He comes, will convict the world concerning sin and righteousness and judgment; concerning sin, because they do not believe in Me; and concerning righteousness, because I go to the Father and you no longer see Me; and concerning judgment, because the ruler of this world has been judged" (John 16:8–11).

Other Christians may be used of God to soften a person toward the Gospel. For example, Philip spoke to the Ethiopian eunuch (Acts 8:26–35) after the Spirit impressed Philip to talk to this man. An obedient Philip preached Jesus to the man, and the man trusted Christ as a result.

Circumstances can be used in a person's life to incline him or her toward the Gospel. For example, after an earthquake shook him up, a Philippian jailer asked, "What must I do to be saved?" (Acts 16:19–34). The Lord is able to use a variety of events in a person's life to turn his attention toward the Gospel. A tragedy may turn people's attention toward the Lord; a hospital stay may wake up a person to what the Lord may be doing in his life.

God also may use you or me as a tool in a person's life. I can remember a professor saying in class that it takes an average of seven contacts with a believer before an unbeliever trusts Christ. I have no idea where those figures come from; however, the point was you play an important part in God's plan. All God is asking is that you be faithful and leave the results in His hands.

FAITHFULNESS IS THE KEY

What counts in evangelism is not numbers for performance, but faithfulness. God is the author of conversion. Success depends ultimately upon God and not us. We do the possible and leave the impossible (conversion) to Him. Titus 3:5 reads, "He saved us, not on the basis of deeds which we have done in righteousness, but according to His mercy, by the washing of regeneration and renewing by the Holy Spirit."

"Success" in evangelism (from our perspective) is to *be faithful to share the Gospel in the power of the Holy Spirit and leave the results to Him.* It has nothing to do with counting widgets or converts; it has everything to do with being faithful. Faithfulness and consistency are what God is asking of us.

William Carey, the great missionary to India, wrote, "If, after my removal, any one should think it worth his while to write my life, I will give you a criterion by which you may judge of its correctness. If he give me credit for being a plodder, he will describe me justly. Anything beyond this will be too much. I can plod. I can persevere in any definite pursuit. To this I owe everything."[5]

> Maybe you feel the temptation to quit.
> Be faithful! Keep plodding!

I can do that! I can plod. I can hang in there. For me, desirable characteristics like faithfulness and consistency in ministry come to mind and encourage me to press on. Proverbs 3:3 says, "Let love and faithfulness never leave you; bind them around your neck, write them on the tablet of your heart" (NIV).

Often in ministry, there is a temptation to retreat rather than persevere. The tendency is to give up when the going gets tough rather than work through the difficulties. For William Carey, I am sure that the pressures of ministry in India, with all the accompanying difficulties, were great, yet he kept plodding. For us, the pressures may come through a variety of different forms, but the feelings are the same. Maybe you feel the temptation to quit. Be faithful! Keep plodding!

The concept of faithfulness is applicable in other areas of life as well. What is success as a student? Is being a good student getting all A's on your report card? Is it graduating with honors? That is what the world would say. And if we are seduced by the world's thinking, we may be tempted to do whatever is necessary to guarantee good grades at the end of the semester. But all that God requires of us is to be faithful. All that God requires is to be faithful to "do [our] work heartily, as for the Lord rather than for men" (Colossians 3:23) and leave the results in His hands.

What is success as a parent? Is being a successful parent having all your children grow up as missionaries? Is it having all your children line up in a row and sing in harmony? The world judges a successful parent by good behavior (whatever that is). However, all that God asks of us is to be faithful to "train up a child in the way he should go" (Proverbs 22:6) and leave the results in His hands.

What is success as a husband? Is it to control your spouse in such a way that she conforms to your every wish? As a wife, is it to finally get your husband to put his clothes in the hamper? That is the way that the world typically judges success. But success in God's eyes is for husbands to be faithful to "love your wives, just as Christ also loved the church" (Ephesians 5:25), and for wives to be faithful to "be subject to your own husbands, as to the Lord" (Ephesians 5:22) and leave the results to God.

What is success as a pastor? Is success as a pastor having the next megachurch? Is success having a radio and tape ministry? Is having the biggest church success? That is the way that the world looks at it. However, God sees what man is not able to see. Success in God's eyes is being faithful to "shepherd the flock of God among you" (1 Peter 5:2) and leave the results to God.

And when we come to evangelism, all that God is asking is that we be faithful.

I know a Christian worker involved in a parachurch ministry of evangelism. He faithfully goes about his business, year after year, without a lot of fanfare and fame. He is a prayer warrior and firmly believes that God is the One in control and will bring the people that He wants to hear the message of salvation. He works hard, mostly behind the scenes, making arrangements and setting up events. Someone asked me about him recently and I had the opportunity to point out that he has been faithfully serving God in this ministry for about thirty years. Each year between four hundred and five hundred people trust Christ as a result of this man's behind-the-scenes efforts. In other words, because of his faithfulness, and his ability to plod, maybe as many as fifteen thousand people are now populating heaven!

Faithfulness will outperform ability in the long run. I can plod. Consistency and faithfulness are keys to any definite pursuit. Are you being faithful?

PART TWO:
PRACTICAL PROCLAMATION

NINE:
ARE YOU PASSIVE OR ACTIVE?

EVANGELISM PRINCIPLE 5: *Being a good witness means passionately pursuing the lost in love.*

IN MARCH 1860 American transportation pioneer William H. Russell placed an advertisement in newspapers. It read, "Wanted: Young, skinny, wiry fellows not over 18. Must be expert riders willing to risk death daily. Orphans preferred."[1]

The many young men who responded to that ad became a part of the American legend called the Pony Express. From April 3, 1860, to October 24, 1861 (when the telegraph was completed), you could send a one-half-ounce letter from St. Joseph, Missouri, to Sacramento, California, for five dollars. It would take about ten days to make the trip—an impressive time, considering the Overland Stage route took twice as long.[2]

Riders were hired in a hurry and had to swear on a Bible not to cuss, fight, or abuse their animals and to conduct themselves honestly. They also had to weigh less than 125 pounds. Riding between seventy-five and one hundred miles each day, they changed horses at relay stations set ten to fifteen miles apart—all for about twenty-five dollars a week.

The Pony Express motto was "The mail must go through." But

the reputation of the express depended upon each rider to carry the mail over that two-thousand-mile central route. It was a vast unknown land primarily inhabited by Native Americans. Those riders became models of determination and courage to America. They delivered the message, no matter what the cost, often through hostile territory.

In much the same way, Jesus has called us to help bring the message of the Gospel to a lost world no matter what the cost.

In Luke 9, Jesus called His first disciples to a high level of commitment. He said to "take nothing" (Luke 9:3). He said that they would encounter hostility (9:5). Some tough discipleship teaching followed (vv. 57–62). Next Jesus instructed seventy other disciples to pray for workers (10:2), and then sent them out in pairs (vv. 1, 3).

The cost may be great. We are called to be models of determination and courage. But how are we going to be able to pull it off? In this section we are talking about the practical proclamation of the Gospel message—taking the Gospel to a lost and at times hostile world. But where do we start?

BEING A GOOD WITNESS

You start by being a good witness for Jesus Christ. But what exactly is a good witness for Jesus Christ? Being a good witness is being salt and light in a tasteless and dark world by living by grace and truth. Being a witness is more involved in cultivating relationships and sowing seeds in the process of disciple making.[3] But being a witness is anything but being passive in life and not being involved with people. *Being a witness is passionately pursuing the lost in love and being intimately involved with people.*

You are a witness for Jesus Christ because of the indwelling of the Holy Spirit in your life. You are to do the work of an evangelist. You can be either a good witness for Jesus Christ or a poor witness for Jesus Christ, but one way or another you are a witness!

Matthew 5:13–16 reads:

You are the salt of the earth; but if the salt has become tasteless, how can it be made salty again? It is no longer good for anything, except to be thrown out and trampled under foot by men. You are the light of the world. A city set on a hill cannot be hidden; nor does anyone light a lamp and put it under a basket, but on the lampstand, and it gives light to all who are in the house. Let your light shine before men in such a way that they may see your good works and glorify your Father who is in heaven.

Notice that the last sentence in these words from Jesus assumes that good works are taking place! "Let your light shine before men in such a way that they may see your good works." When believers accomplish good works, unbelievers in turn marvel at our God!

"I planted, Apollos watered, but God was causing the growth," Paul wrote in 1 Corinthians 3:6. Farmers will tell you that planting, watering, and harvesting are not passive tasks. There is work associated with each activity. You first have to cultivate the soil. Then you sow the seeds and make sure that the seeds have the right nourishment and water to grow. There is no sitting back and waiting for things to happen; there is effort involved.

I think Paul exemplified what it means to be a witness in 1 Thessalonians 2:1–12. Paul and Silas had been released from the Philippian jail (Acts 16:12; 17:1–3) and they came to Thessalonica. Paul even referenced his time in Philippi as he underscored his pure motives in coming to the Thessalonians. "After we had already suffered and been mistreated in Philippi, as you know, we had the boldness in our God to speak to you the gospel of God amid much opposition" (1 Thessalonians 2:2).

Their ministry did not spring from trying to bait or trick people (v. 3), but was pure in motive. They were not interested in "pleasing men, but God" (v. 4).

Paul and Silas were not seeking glory from men (v. 6), but instead, "proved to be gentle among you, as a nursing mother tenderly cares for her own children" (v. 7).

Think about a nursing mother tenderly caring for her own child. She is loving. She is very protective of her child and knows that baby's needs. In fact, it seems that she can tell when that baby is hungry, wet, or hurt by the type of cry that the baby makes.

That mother is also very sacrificial. She is willing to do anything that is necessary for the well-being of that child. She will get up in the middle of the night to minister to the needs of the child. She will sacrifice herself for the sake of the child.

Now, let me ask you a question. Paul and Silas proved to the Thessalonians that they had those characteristics of a nursing mother. Is that passive or is that active? They were *actively* involved in the Thessalonians' lives. There was nothing passive about their ministry!

In fact, Paul added, "You are witnesses, and so is God, how devoutly and uprightly and blamelessly we behaved toward you believers" (v. 10). And it was for this very reason that when the Thessalonians received the word of God's message, they "accepted it not as the word of men, but for what is really is, the word of God" (v. 13).

What a witness for Jesus Christ! They proved by their lives that they were believers. The works that they did caused the Thessalonians to glorify God in heaven. They were passionately pursuing the lost in love. There was nothing passive about Paul and Silas' lives. They were actively involved in the lives of the Thessalonians.

Being a witness means passionately pursuing the lost in love.

Paul and Silas were not just living in the neighborhood waiting for people to come up and ask them about Jesus. They were proving the same characteristics that a nursing mother demonstrates to her child. They were sacrificial, loving, and attentive to each individual's needs. The Thessalonians were able to witness that type of behavior and respond.

In his book *Gentle Persuasion,* Joe Aldrich wrote, "As I read the Scriptures, I'm haunted by the idea that God is not so much asking you to tell your people what a friend they have in Jesus, as in showing them what a friend they have in you."[4] Showing an unbeliever love takes sacrifice—the same sacrifice that Paul was able to show the Thessalonians.

What does it mean to be a good witness? It begins with a very simple premise. Sharing the gospel of Jesus Christ with a lost world is not a passive activity but an active activity. Being a witness for Jesus Christ means passionately pursuing the lost in love. Being a witness does not mean badgering the lost, but you can pursue them in love.

Where are your Thessalonians? Who are those people that you are demonstrating the Gospel to in the same way that Paul and Silas were demonstrating the Gospel to the Thessalonians?

Whenever I hear someone say, "Well, I am into relational strategies," I have to think in my mind, *Super! Where are your Thessalonians? Point them out to me.* I want them to show me the people they are ministering to in the same way that Paul was ministering to the Thessalonians.

In today's Christian culture, many of us have equated being a witness with passivity and inactivity. We seem to have the idea that if we just quietly live our lives, people will automatically come up to us and ask about Jesus Christ. However, as I look in Scripture and read about the relationships that Paul had with individuals, there was nothing passive about their relationships at all!

How can I passionately pursue people in love? How can I get involved in people's lives to be able to start leveraging them toward the Gospel? The answer is practicing three forms of witness.

THREE KINDS OF WITNESSES

There are really three forms of being a witness for Jesus Christ. We can be (1) a life witness, (2) a verbal witness, and (3) a corporate witness.

Being a witness gives testimony to the relationship that we enjoy with Jesus Christ. We can be or give a testimony about Jesus Christ without actually sharing the Gospel. Evangelism is the communication of the good news of Jesus Christ with the intent of inviting the listener to trust Christ. Being a witness is not evangelism, but is a way to open the door to evangelism. Being a witness builds a bridge into an unbeliever's life so that the Gospel may be shared in the future.

Each kind of witness can use a number of different approaches; however, no witness is passive or inactive in life. All are passionately pursuing the lost in love.

BEING A LIFE WITNESS

A life witness depends on a positive lifestyle. How you live your life should be a testimony of your relationship with Jesus Christ. There are a number of ways that you can live your life for Jesus Christ and be a testimony for your Lord.

First, you can be a witness merely by your presence. In the hospital, a part of the witness that I have in that environment is my presence. I wear a badge that indicates that I am a chaplain in the hospital. And how I conduct myself as an ambassador for Jesus Christ can be a positive or negative witness for Him. Paul was a tent maker and obviously worked among the people while sharing the Gospel so as not to be a burden to anyone (1 Thessalonians 2:9; 2 Thessalonians 3:8). His presence among the people gave him a platform from which to proclaim the Gospel.

But anyone can have a witness of presence. How you conduct yourself in the marketplace or how you treat your neighbors can be a testimony to the reality of the Lord in your life. But, once again, remember that being a witness for Jesus Christ is not evangelism. Being a witness is a bridge to be able to share the Gospel.

Second, you can be a life witness through acts of service. Someone who mows his neighbor's lawn, washes his car, takes care of his dog, fixes a fence, or even takes out his garbage is performing an act of ser-vice. Such activities are not so much associated with Christianity but with going out of one's way to show kindness to an individual.[5] In Acts 6, the disciples had to choose seven men of good reputation to be put in charge of the task of the daily serving of food. I am sure that their acts of service to the larger community drew many to the Savior.

Hopefully, as you show kindness in unexpected and extravagant means, an individual will be softened to the Gospel. Mowing some-one's lawn is not the Gospel, but it is a bridge to be able to share the Gospel.

Third, you can be a life witness through acts of Christian service. Such acts are linked with Christianity and might include a church that has organized a clothes closet or food pantry to assist individuals in the community. Under the banner of Christianity, the church is able to provide clothes and food to those who have need. Stephen was "per-forming great wonders and signs among the people" (Acts 6:8), to the point where he was brought before the Council for his activities. They had no doubt that his testimony and good works were all for the sake of Jesus.

Other examples might be a ministry to the itinerant, to the home-less, to abandoned kids, or to unwed mothers. All of these acts of ser-vice are associated with a Christian word or witness. Once again, these acts of Christian service are not the Gospel, but they are bridges into an individual's life to be able to share the Gospel.

BEING A VERBAL WITNESS

Not only do we have the opportunity to be a witness for Jesus Christ through our lives, but we also can give testimony to the power of Jesus Christ verbally. Giving a verbal testimony to God's power in our lives is not the Gospel. It is just what it is: It is giving testimony to Christ's power in our lives. That can happen a number of different ways.

First, a verbal witness could come in the form of a faith story. This might be a testimony of how God has worked in your past. You might be able to give a testimony of how faithful God has been and how you know that He will be faithful in the future.

As I went through seminary, God was faithful to meet our family's needs. I was able to see Him work in amazing ways to make it possible to pay the monthly bills. When we were coming to the end of our seminary experience, it was easy to rest and be content in Him. We were able to look back and know that as God had been faithful in bringing us that far, He would certainly prove Himself faithful in providing an opportunity to serve.

These faith stories are a verbal testimony to God working in your life. Again, they are not the Gospel; they are a bridge to be able to share the Gospel. I might be able to share the most powerful faith story possible, but if I never get around to sharing the good news about Jesus Christ, that person is still lost!

There was our opportunity to tell
the person how God was central to our family.

A second way to be a verbal witness is by offering belief and value statements. Such statements have been called "raising the flag,"[6] letting people know that you are a Christian by some statement that reveals your values or basis of authority. You might be able to give value statements about your priorities in life or your goals in raising your children. Belief and value statements reveal why you do what you do. In other words, the reason that you hold to this position, or the reason that you believe this has happened in your life, is because you are a Christian.

We have been able to have a lot of fun with belief and value statements in our family. Back when Tim was playing baseball, Patty was sitting in the stands with one of the other moms. The conversation turned to the number of children in our family, and when Patty told the woman we had four children, she was amazed that our children were all from the same couple. We were odd. We were the only family that was not a "blended" family on that baseball team.

This revelation about our family quickly made its way around the team. Everybody was now watching our family. Questions started coming on a variety of issues, from our longstanding marriage to family and on to kids. Those questions gave us some opportunities to raise the flag of Christianity with belief and value statements.

"How do you raise your kids?" someone might ask. Up went the flag. "We have only three goals for our kids—independence from parents, dependence upon God, and responsibility for their own actions."

"Dependence upon God?" the person would often question. And there was our opportunity to tell the person how God was central to our family and our personal lives.

Other opportunities have arisen in our family to raise the flag of Christianity. As my older daughter was getting up to dating age, I was faced with the prospect of some young man coming to the door to take her out on a date.

I needed some way to be able to communicate my values to that young man. So, I came up with what is affectionately called in our family the "three nothings." The three nothings are: nothing below the neck, nothing comes off, and nothing lying down.

Now before a young man took out my daughter, he usually would come over for dinner. Before he came I would ask my daughter, "Would you like to tell him the three nothings, or would you like for me to tell him the three nothings?" Usually my daughter would tell him the three nothings before he arrived at our door. However, that gave me a good opportunity when we met to merely ask the young man, "I am sure that my daughter has told you about the three nothings?"

"Yes, sir."

"Good. What are they?" I would ask.

"Nothing below the neck. Nothing comes off. And nothing lying down."

"Super!" I would reply. "I just want you to know that I know them. My daughter knows them and you know them. However, I am holding you responsible."

Now you may think that this is cruel, but let me tell you how this has worked in my family. Usually young girls talk about dating way before the first date comes along. Our children were no different. Many of those conversations revolved around the three nothings. The three nothings often led to opportunities to share about the centrality of Jesus Christ in a relationship, which led to talking about a personal relationship with Jesus Christ. This all happened through belief and value statements, answering the question of why we do what we do.

I was doing some premarital counseling with a young couple who was new to the church. In the first session I asked them if they had established any boundaries in their physical expression during their engagement period. They had not talked about the subject and asked if I had any suggestions. I told them the three nothings, after which the young lady turned to the young man and said, "Well, strike three!" That gave me the opportunity to help that young couple establish some boundaries and talk about the good news of Jesus Christ.

> Value statements ... form bridges into
> people's lives by expressing why we do what we do.

We also gave our children purity rings. At Christmas of their freshman year in high school, we gave each of our kids a ring. Each child was required to take a vow of purity that read: "With this ring, I promise to remain pure. Before God and my family, I promise to wear this ring, a symbol of my vow, until this ring is replaced by the ring of my husband. In the name of the Father, the Son, and the Holy Spirit, Amen."

With such a simple symbol like a purity ring, our kids have had a number of opportunities to share the good news about Jesus Christ. Often the conversation will begin with a comment like, "Wow, I wish that I had a family that cared about me like that!"

All of these are simply belief and value statements. They form bridges into people's lives by expressing why we do what we do. They raise the flag of Christianity and provide an opportunity to talk about spiritual things. They are not the Gospel, but are a witness to the power of the living Christ in our lives.

A third kind of verbal witness might be in the form of an evangelistic Bible study—a study of Scripture on a particular passage or topic that sparks an interest in spiritual things among those in attendance. This could be a book of the Bible, or it could center on a particular topic that is discussed in Scripture. Many topics may be of interest to your unbelieving friends. A topic like marriage, money, or the family might be interesting to your neighbors or coworkers.

The study not only gives directions for life, but it also provides a vehicle for spiritual things to be discussed. Typically the Bible study does not focus on the Gospel but provides a bridge for sharing the Gospel. You are giving a verbal witness to life that is found in Jesus Christ.

BEING A CORPORATE WITNESS

Another form of being a witness is through the church itself—being a corporate witness. The love that we show for one another is a form of a witness to the lost world. Jesus said, "By this all men will know that you are My disciples, if you have love for one another" (John 13:35).

The way that we treat one another can be a good witness—or a bad witness—to the world. Either way, we do have a witness to the world. Many are the churches who have lost their positive witness in their community through a poor testimony. Gossip, coolness to visitors, even a poorly maintained property can foster a bad testimony with the community.

Of course, many churches do relate well to their neighborhood and have a positive witness for Jesus Christ. It could be going out of our way to make sure that we are good neighbors to the community. Any way that you slice it, we do have a witness for Jesus Christ.

Our relationship with other brothers and sisters in Christ not only becomes a witness to a lost world, but it also helps to stimulate us toward greater fruitfulness for Jesus Christ (Hebrews 10:24–25). Jim Petersen wrote,

> God never intended evangelism to be an individualistic effort. The biblical pattern is for the individual's witness to be carried on within the setting of a corporate effort. The corporate witness says, "Look at all of us. This is what you too can become. There's hope." It's possible to discount or explain away an isolated individual, but it's impossible to refute the corporate testimony. The Apostle John observed, "No one has ever seen God; but if we love one another, God lives in us and his love is made complete in us" (1 John 4:12 [NIV]).[7]

Being a good witness for Jesus Christ is passionately pursuing the lost in love. You can be a witness for Jesus Christ through your life, in verbal opportunities, or in your relationship with other believers. Being a witness is giving testimony to what Christ has done in your life.

TEN:
BECOMING REAL

MY WIFE AND I have a number of favorite books that we read to our children. Among them is *The Velveteen Rabbit,* a story about some toys that live in a nursery. One of my favorite exchanges in the book happens between the Rabbit and the Skin Horse.

> Between them all the poor little Rabbit was made to feel himself very insignificant and commonplace, and the only person who was kind to him at all was the Skin Horse. . . .
>
> "What is REAL?" asked the Rabbit one day, when they were lying side by side near the nursery fender, before Nana came to tidy the room. "Does it mean having things that buzz inside you and a stick-out handle?"
>
> "Real isn't how you are made," said the Skin Horse. "It's a thing that happens to you. When a child loves you for a long, long time, not just to play with, but REALLY loves you, then you become Real."
>
> "Does it hurt?" asked the Rabbit.
>
> "Sometimes," said the Skin Horse, for he was always truthful. "When you are Real you don't mind being hurt."

"Does it happen all at once, like being wound up," he asked, "or bit by bit?"

"It doesn't happen all at once," said the Skin Horse. "You become. It takes a long time. That's why it doesn't often happen to people who break easily, or have sharp edges, or who have to be carefully kept. Generally, by the time you are Real, most of your hair has been loved off, and your eyes drop out and you get loose in the joints and very shabby. But these things don't matter at all, because once you are Real you can't be ugly, except to people who don't understand."[1]

In evangelism it is our job to become REAL to people in the world. But just like the story, we often see a number of "bells and whistles" come onto the scene—things that "buzz inside you" or "a stick-out handle"—offering some new gimmick, a new method, or some new way to approach evangelism. But they are just passing fads and will never turn into anything else.

Becoming real in *The Velveteen Rabbit* doesn't often happen to "people who break easily, or have sharp edges, or who have to be carefully kept." We are just like that. Becoming real is going to require sacrifice on our part. It is going to mean unconditional love to love the unlovely people of the world. But how specifically is that going to happen? Paul gives us a little insight in 1 Corinthians 9:1–23.

In talking to the Corinthians, the apostle Paul is using himself as a positive example of how to exercise freedom. In chapter 8, Paul declared that he would be willing to give up some of his rights if it would prevent a brother from stumbling (8:13). Now Paul expands that thought and illustrates that principle by relating it to the issue of support. Paul refused to be supported by those he ministered to because he did not want to be accused of being motivated by money. Paul's desire was to "offer the gospel without charge" (9:18). Paul chose to exercise his freedom in this area. In developing his argument, we see three choices that it takes to become real to people.

BECOMING REAL
BY ABANDONING RIGHTS

First, to become real requires an abandonment of some of our rights. Paul asks a series of questions: "Do we not have a *right* to eat and drink? Do we not have a *right* to take along a believing wife . . . ? Or do only Barnabas and I not have a *right* to refrain from working? . . . If others share the *right* over you, do we not more?" (1 Corinthians 9:4–6, 12, all italics added). Then he explains, "Nevertheless, we did not use this *right,* but we endure all things so that we will cause no hindrance to the gospel of Christ." In verse 18, he explains why he rejects payment: "That when I preach the gospel, I may offer the gospel without charge, so as not to make full use of my *right* in the gospel" (italics added). To become real to people is going to take an abandonment of some of our rights.

In contrast, we are encouraged in today's society to stand up for our rights, even to demand our rights. If our rights are denied, we feel slighted. Television advertisers make sure that we are continually reminded of our rights. In fact, their battle cry to us is, "You deserve it. . . . Go ahead; pamper yourself!"

However, Paul was willing to give up his rights for the sake of the Gospel. Similarly we need to make some sacrifice if we plan to become real to unbelievers. We may need to get up off the couch and engage unbelievers. Even though I might have earned the right to sit here and watch television, I am willing to give up that right to help my neighbor fix his fence. Even though I have earned the right to have a break today, I am willing to give up that right to minister to another person. It is going to take some sacrifice for the sake of the Gospel.

BECOMING REAL
BY ACCEPTING RESPONSIBILITY

Second, to become real requires an acceptance of responsibility. Paul wrote, "For if I preach the gospel, I have nothing to boast of, for

131

I am under compulsion; for woe is me if I do not preach the gospel" (1 Corinthians 9:16). The apostle realized that it was his responsibility to engage the unbeliever with the good news of Jesus Christ.

This principle also is contrary to the world's view: "Someone else will do it. . . . And if something goes wrong, somebody else was responsible." *After all,* we reason, *it is not our responsibility.* But Paul accepted the responsibility and realized that if the Gospel was going to go forth, then he was going to have to be the one who brought it about.

Becoming real to people means putting faith into action, accepting our responsibility to engage unbelievers with the good news of Jesus Christ. Each of us needs to take the responsibility to get involved in a person's life and not wait for someone else. This may mean that I need to make time in my schedule to volunteer at a local homeless shelter or participate in the evangelism ministry at church.

The point is, you and I need to take the responsibility to get involved somewhere.

BECOMING REAL
BY ACTING AS SERVANTS

Third, to become real requires the adoption of a servant's role. Paul wrote, "For though I am free from all men, I have made myself a slave to all, so that I may win more" (v. 19). He later explained, "To the weak I became weak, that I might win the weak; I have become all things to all men, so that I may by all means save some. I do all things for the sake of the gospel, so that I may become a fellow partaker of it" (verses 22–23). Paul willingly adopted a servant's role for the sake of the Gospel. If we are going to become real, we need to adopt a servant's role.

A few years ago one group in my evangelism course decided the best way to become real in a distance runner's life was to offer foot massages after the race. So they found the local 5K and 10K (kilometer) races, set up a tent, and began to offer foot massages, merely as a way to build a bridge to share the Gospel. Talk about adopting a servant's role. Would you be willing to massage feet in order to share the Gospel? Paul was willing to "become all things to all men" and women for the sake of the Gospel. Is that our attitude?

If we can answer yes, the next question is, How do we do that? Where do we start?

GET INVOLVED IN SERVICE
AND MINISTRY TO UNBELIEVERS

The answer is simple: Have regular, consistent contact with unbelievers. There is no impact without contact.

This seems fairly obvious; however, this basic principle is often overlooked. You need to be in contact with unbelievers in order to reach them with the Gospel. Develop an outreach attitude. Look for ways to get involved in individuals' lives. Be willing to do more than just engage in a conversation; be willing to enter a life. This requires your abandoning some of your rights, accepting responsibility, and adopting a servant's role.

You might be saying right now, "But I do not have any contact with unbelievers!" My answer: What is it that you like to do?

Evangelism does not have to take place "out there" somewhere. Yet many of us believe that being a witness and doing evangelism has to be drudgery and something we must force ourselves to do. Instead, why not see the disciple-making process as a part of your recreational life?

Some time ago a student complained to me that he had limited time and there was "no way" that he could spend time with unbelievers. I asked him, "What do you like to do?" I found out that he had been a basketball player in his first year of college until a knee injury forced him to quit. However, he still had a passion for the game and found basketball to be a wonderful recreational activity.

"Have you ever considered using basketball as a bridge into people's lives?" I asked. "Is there a way to be able to give away your passion and your talents to someone else?"

Weeks later that young man came to see me. He had heard me, and for the past six weeks he had held a basketball clinic for eight- to ten-year-old boys on Saturday mornings at a local community center. He had met with these boys for a couple of hours each week. The boys thought that he was a basketball legend! He enjoyed the opportunity to give away some of his skills. He also had a great time with the contact and the recreation. Not only did he get to know a bunch of young boys but also the parents who brought them to the clinic and picked them up every Saturday.

What is it that you like to do? What can you give away? You need to get involved with unbelievers on a regular basis. That is the place to start. Do you have a hobby? Do you have an interest? Whatever hobby or interest you have, there is probably a club in your area with people who have the same interests. All it requires is the initiative to get involved.

Maybe you have always wanted to learn about a particular skill or hobby. All it is going to take is getting involved in a club or taking a class. I have a whole list of things that I would like to do someday. I know very little about photography, but I would sure like to take a class in photography. I might even try oil painting someday! I would love to learn to oil paint, and I am sure that there is someone out there who would love to get me involved. All it will require is for me to show a little interest.

> Evangelism is a
> contact sport.

For my son-in-law's twenty-fifth birthday, he decided he wanted to go sky diving. My daughter found a sky diving club outside Dallas and set up the date. We all went out to watch him jump from the plane. While we were out at the airport awaiting his big jump, I had the opportunity to get into a conversation with a sky diving enthusi-ast. He was an accountant all week in Dallas, and during the weekends he would park his recreational vehicle at the airport and sky dive. On Sunday afternoon he would drive back to Dallas and start the cycle over again.

As I talked with this gentleman, it struck me that if I was really in-terested in sky diving, here would be a perfect opportunity to bridge into his life. If I walked into that place and announced that I wanted to learn all about sky diving, I would probably have a dozen or so peo-ple scrambling for my attention. It would have been easy to break into that little mini-subculture of America.

What are you interested in? What would you like to learn? What skills would you like to give away? Maybe you are interested in sports, woodworking, sewing, or gardening. Possibly you are a jogger or are looking into a new hobby or interest. Are there opportunities for you to be involved in a club or activity center that would help encourage your interest?

There is no impact without contact. Evangelism is a contact sport. You need to be involved in regular and consistent contact with unbe-lievers. Make it fun! Do something that you are interested in! Make it a part of your normal recreational activity.

CLARIFY YOUR PERSONAL STRATEGY

Clarifying exactly what you are trying to do in the conversion pro-cess often helps to free people for ministry. This starts with a basic understanding of strategies. A strategy of evangelism is the means by which evangelism takes place. As we said in an earlier chapter, the strategy is not evangelism. It is a vehicle for evangelism to happen. A strategy includes both witnessing and evangelism. It is a *blending* of our walk and our talk to ultimately share the Gospel with an unbeliever.

We seem to have created a tension between two different strategies of evangelism—aggressive strategies and relational strategies. It seems to be almost an either/or type of mentality that we carry, rather than some mixture of a both/and mentality. How do these strategies fit together?

The aggressive strategy of evangelism relies more on your talk than on your walk. The emphasis in this strategy is on the proclamation of the Good News. Those individuals who are part of this camp usually place a high emphasis on the harvest of the unbelievers and speak very little about cultivation. They do speak about cultivation; however, they seem to emphasize the harvest. You can witness with your walk, but you cannot evangelize. With your talk you can both witness and evangelize.

As we talk about aggressive strategies, we need to remember that some people do respond to the Good News the first time that they hear it. God is preparing the hearts of people to respond to the truth. Two clear examples in Acts are Philip speaking with the Ethiopian eunuch (8:29–39) and Paul speaking with King Agrippa (26:1–32).

The relational strategy of evangelism relies more upon your walk than on your talk. The emphasis is on loving, serving, and modeling the Christian life in order to make Christianity attractive to an unbeliever. The relational strategy only becomes an evangelistic strategy as the loving, serving, and modeling leads to an opportunity to share the Gospel. Those individuals who are a part of this camp usually place a high emphasis on the cultivation of unbelievers and speak very little about the harvest. They do speak about the harvest; however, they emphasize the cultivation.

It appears that few people in the church really know how to make friends with unbelievers and then turn those friendships into opportunities to share the Gospel. When you employ the relational strategy, remember that if you love people without ever getting around to preaching the good news of Jesus Christ, those unbelievers are still lost. *All relational strategies must become aggressive strategies somewhere along the line, or you are not properly utilizing the relational strategy.* Relational strategies are not an excuse for inactivity and passivity, but are a means for evangelism to take place.

But what strategy should I use? How should I determine how much of my strategy should rely upon my walk, and how much should rely upon my talk? Is it arbitrary?

> The closer my relationship is . . .
> the more relational my strategy should be.

The average believer sometimes is confused as to how this all fits together. After all, Scripture commands us to do the work of an evangelist (2 Timothy 4:5). Yet in 1 Peter 3:1–2 the apostle instructs the wife who is married to an unbelieving husband to remain silent and be more relational in her strategy. She is to rely almost totally upon her walk and win her husband to the Lord without her talk. And the apostle Paul appears to demonstrate an attitude somewhere in between in 1 Thessalonians 2:1–12.

Scriptures seem to set before us the criterion that the nature of our relationship with a person is the deciding factor in whether to be more relational in our strategy or more aggressive in our strategy. It appears that *the closer my relationship is with an individual, the more relational my strategy should be. The more casual the relationship that I have with an individual, the more aggressive in my strategy I have to be.*[2] In other words, with the people who are able to watch how I live (my walk), I have the ability to practically demonstrate the love of the Gospel. With people with whom I do not have a close relationship, I need to use more of my talk because they are not able to see the quality of my walk.

Consider the example of Paul with the Thessalonians (1 Thessalonians 2) versus Paul with the Athenians (Acts 17). He adapted his approach to the people, depending on his relationship with them. In the case of the Thessalonians, whom he knew well, Paul was very relational in his strategy. In the case of the Athenians, whom he knew much less, he was very aggressive in his strategy.

Other times, Paul used his ability to reason and argue for the faith. Paul was "reasoning" with the Jews in the synagogue and with the Gentiles in the marketplace every day in Athens (Acts 17:17). When Paul was in Ephesus he "reasoned daily in the school of Tyrannus" (Acts 19:9).

Figure 5 shows the correspondence between aggressive and relational strategies. The more casual the relationship that I have with an individual, the more aggressive the strategy needs to be. It does not mean that I will not be relational at all; however, I will rely more upon my talk than my walk. On the other side of the spectrum, the closer the relationship that I have with an individual, the more relational I am able to be. Eventually, I will need to become aggressive and rely upon my talk to share the Gospel; however, because of the nature of my relationship with this person, I am able to rely more upon my walk to communicate God's love.

WHICH STRATEGY WITH YOUR PARENTS?

Let's consider a few examples that may help to clarify this principle. Let's say that you desire to share the Gospel with your parents. What would be the most appropriate strategy to approach your parents with the Gospel? Should you rely more upon your talk to share the Gospel or rely more upon your walk to soften them to the Gospel?

With your parents, the most appropriate strategy is to be more relational. Why? Because the relationship with one's parents is very close, that is, they tend to know us well; they have had the opportunity to watch and observe our lifestyle for years.

We probably do our young people a disservice in our evangelism training when we suggest to them that they go home and share the Gospel with their parents using an aggressive strategy. Now there is nothing wrong with an aggressive strategy; however, with their parents it probably will not be the wisest way to approach them with the Good News.

Figure 5

ADOPTING YOUR STRATEGY

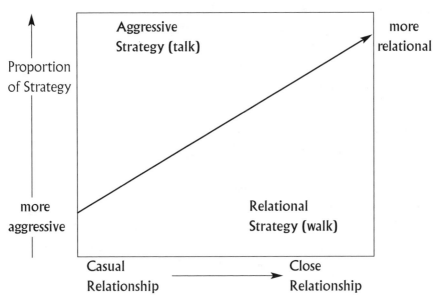

Picture the scene. A youngster, all eager to share the Gospel with his folks, gathers them into the living room and proudly announces that he has some news for them. The bad news is that they are both sinners. The bad news gets worse as they find out that the wages of their sin is death, eternal separation from God. The Good News is that Christ died for their sin and arose from the dead, and that all that they need to do is to trust Him for forgiveness of their sins. At this point the young person asks, "Is there anything that is keeping you from placing your trust in Jesus Christ?" to which his parents reply, "Yes! . . . YOU!! You talk about a sinner! We have known you since the beginning, and you take the cake!"

It might have been better to say to that young person during his evangelism training, "You know, if you want to share the Gospel with your parents, the best way to go about it might be to go home and clean your room for a week. What do you think is going to happen after a week of cleaning your room? Your mother is going to come in and ask, 'What's the matter with you?' Then you will be able to explain the change that has happened in your life. You will be able to demonstrate to them the reality of Jesus Christ in your life." (Or, if you have been a Christian for years, how God has been convicting you about becoming a more obedient son or daughter.) The closer the relationship that you have with an individual, the more relational your strategy can be.

WHICH STRATEGY WITH A STRANGER OR ACQUAINTANCE?

On the other hand, what would be appropriate with someone that you meet on an airplane? The most appropriate strategy on an airplane is to use a more aggressive strategy. You will need to rely more upon your talk than your walk. Why? Because you are both strapped to an airplane! That individual does not have a clue about what a wonderful person you are! He is unable to observe how you live your life. The only thing that you have to rely upon during that situation is your talk.

That does not mean that you need to be obnoxious or offensive to that person. But you can, if the Lord permits, direct that conversation to spiritual things and passionately pursue that individual to find out where he is in his relationship with Jesus Christ.

In those situations, I have pre-decided the most appropriate strategy and know which direction the conversation will go if I am able to have any influence on the discussion. I merely start asking an individual a broad, general question. I talk about his family. I talk about his occupation and anything else that may be of interest to him. Some of the topics that you may want to pursue include: vacation, hobbies, sports, recreational activities, children, or family interests. Sometimes my occupation comes up, which provides a natural introduction into spiritual things. However, I may need to pursue him a little further to discern his spiritual temperature.

To break the ice on a spiritual conversation I merely ask, "May I ask you a spiritual question?"[3] After all, by then we have probably talked about his family, work, and a host of other topics. After receiving an affirmative response (I have never had anyone say no to that question), I will proceed to ask him another question, "Where are you spiritually?" or "Where are you in your spiritual journey?"

Most often I get the response, "What do you mean?"

"Have you ever come to the place in your spiritual journey where you established a personal relationship with Jesus Christ, or would you say that you are still on the way?"

"I'm still on the way."

"Well, maybe the next step that God might have for you is to come to an understanding of how you can establish a personal relationship with Jesus Christ. Has anyone ever taken a Bible and shown you how you can establish a relationship with Him?"

"No."

"May I?"

ASKING PERMISSION TO CONTINUE

Notice that I have asked permission to continue four different times. In other words, the person whom I am talking to has the opportunity to shut off the conversation four different times. It provides me with the opportunity to try to discern his spiritual temperature.

I look at this initial process as "throwing bread on the water." When we go to the park, sometimes we will take bread to feed the ducks. We stand at the shore and throw a couple of crumbs on top of the water to see if any of the ducks decide to come over to eat. If they do, we throw more bread on the water.

With unbelievers, I always like to throw a few bread crumbs on "top of the water" to see if anyone decides to bite. If they do, I will throw more bread crumbs. If not, I stop throwing crumbs. It is the same process with the message of the Gospel. I will throw a few spiritual questions out there to see if anyone bites. If they do, I will pursue them a little further and continue to throw more pieces of bread. If not, I stop.

WHICH STRATEGY WITH A NEIGHBOR?

Let's try another strategy example. What would be the best strategy to use with your neighbor? Most folks will jump at that question to answer, "Relational!" However, it really depends upon the nature of your relationship with your neighbor! You may have more of an opportunity to be relational with a neighbor who lives next door. Maybe with your neighbor next door you have a number of things in common. He may have lived there for many years. His kids may play with your kids and you share a common property line. However, with the neighbor who lives across the street you may have less in common. You may never see him because he exits through the alley in the back. You may never have had the opportunity to visit. The neighbor across the street does not have an opportunity to see how you live your life. The only thing you have to rely upon during your infrequent visits is your talk and not your walk. The next time you have to get together with that neighbor, your talk is the only thing that you can rely upon because he has never been able to watch your walk.

I read an illustration some time ago that posed a hypothetical dilemma. Suppose that you wake up early on a subzero temperature morning to prepare for an outdoor hike. You are faced with the question, Shall I wear my thermal underwear or shall I wear my coat? To adequately prepare for the weather outside, the answer is, "Wear both!" It is not an either/or question, but it is a both/and question.

As I prepare to enter the world to share the Gospel, should I be more relational or more aggressive in my strategy? In order to be adequately prepared for every situation, the answer is "both!" Evangelism strategies do not depend upon my personal preferences; they depend upon my relationship with an individual. Similarly, with our neighbors, we had better be ready with both, for as our relationships vary from neighbor to neighbor, so should our strategies.

Now let me ask you a very difficult question. Out of the number of relationships that you have, how many are truly close relationships where an individual has the opportunity to watch how you live your life? How many are casual relationships?

CHOOSING THE AGGRESSIVE STRATEGY

I believe that because we all feel more comfortable using the relational strategy, we have fooled ourselves into thinking that the relational strategy is appropriate for every relationship. That may or may not be true. I think that if we were brutally honest with ourselves about the nature of our relationships with people, we would find out that the number of close relationships that we have with people is very few. The church needs to be encouraged to move more of our relationships from casual to close.

The majority of the relationships that I have with people are casual. If I was being honest and looked at the casual nature of my relationships, which strategy is more appropriate and which is the one that I will be using most of the time? For most of our relationships, aggressive strategies are more appropriate.

I once knew a farmer who hired migrant workers every year to help harvest the crop. He was extremely evangelistic, and many of those workers came to know Christ. I asked him how he did it. His response was fascinating. He said that he shared the Gospel with each worker during the interview. He wanted them to know where he stood right from the beginning. He also knew that if he did not take the initiative to share the Gospel at the interview, it would probably be more difficult later. If they did not trust Christ during the interview, he knew that they would be watching his every move. Later he often had an opportunity to share the Gospel again as they had questions or were drawn to the Savior by his walk.

This is a great example of blending one's walk and one's talk. As those workers came for an interview, my friend knew that the relationship was very casual, so he took the initiative to share the Gospel. If they did not trust Christ during the interview, he had the opportunity to witness to them more through his walk, looking for the opportunity to share the Gospel verbally once again.

Relationships are often like that. They start casual and verbal, move closer and become more nonverbal, and then eventually come back to verbal as the Gospel is shared.

CHOOSING *YOUR* STRATEGY

Have you already decided how you are going to relate to individuals? Have you pre-decided to relate to them not so much on the basis of their needs and the nature of your relationship, but rather on the basis of your personal preferences?

Becoming real to people may require you to abandon some of your rights, accept your responsibility, and adopt a servant's role as you get involved in ministry and service with unbelievers. The closer the relationship with an individual, the more relational in your strategy you can be. The more casual the relationship that you have with an individual, the more aggressive in your strategy you have to be. May God use you to become real to the people around you.

ELEVEN:
SEND IN
THE HERO!

EVANGELISM PRINCIPLE 6: *Evangelism moves forward as God's people get involved in ministry and service.*

IT HAS BECOME almost an annual event in the Cecil household to attend the local Mesquite Rodeo at least once a season. The bull-riding event is always a big crowd favorite—and ours too. Eight seconds of drama as some little guy tries to take on a totally out-of-control bull. But usually the eight seconds are only half the fun. The real fun begins as the clowns and cowboys try to herd that bull back into the corral.

Every once in a while they get a really persnickety bull that will not want to go back to the corral. The cowboys will first try to shoo the bull back through the gate. If that doesn't work, a lone cowboy on a horse will lasso the bull and try to drag it back to the corral. If that does not work, they are left with one lone stubborn bull on one end of the arena that is looking at the cowboys almost in defiance, daring anyone to come close. The crowd is wondering what they will do to get this massive, stubborn bull back into the corral.

The trick that they use in this situation is to release *more* bulls into the arena! They bring in about six bulls and drive them down to the far side where that stubborn bull is standing. The stubborn one mixes in with the rest of the herd and the cowboys easily drive the whole herd out of the arena and into the corral. The once stubborn, mighty, and usually mad bull calms down and becomes just one of the crowd. The herd mentality at work!

In evangelism, we can almost become just like that persnickety bull. When we begin to think of evangelism only in individual terms, we are setting ourselves up for frustration. We begin to take on the entire responsibility for the world ourselves. Being a Lone Ranger in evangelism can lead to frustration and anger. Unfortunately, we can become isolated and not accountable to anyone when we focus on "doing our own thing." In some cases, I can become mad. I can feel alone, alienated, and just plain stubborn. So what is the cure? Send in the herd! The cure is to let some more bulls into the arena! The cure is to expand my vision past the "just them and me" attitude.

NEVER ALONE

While we have the commandment to go into the world, we must balance our thinking with the reality that we were never created to operate totally alone. The image of God is fully reflected in plurality.

The book of Genesis contains the creation account. In Genesis 1:3, God created the light. After creating the light, "God saw that the light was good" (Genesis 1:4). God continued as He created the land and the seas and once again pronounced that "it was good" (1:10). He created the vegetation, plants, and trees and "saw that it was good" (1:12). He created the sun, moon, and stars and "saw that it was good" (1:18). He went on to create every living creature that moves and every winged bird and once again "saw that it was good" (1:21). He brought forth the cattle and creeping things and "saw that it was good" (1:25). And then "God saw all that He had made, and behold, it was very good" (1:31).

But when you skip over to Genesis 2:18, after creating man God states, "It is not good for the man to be alone; I will make him a helper suitable for him." What in the world could not be good about man being alone? Adam had it made! He lived in a perfect world. He had everything that someone could ask for. He had job security and was the CEO of the kingdom! Plus, Adam had a perfect relationship with God! What in the world could not be going right? Isn't this the type of setting that we all long for?

Yet God says that the situation is not good. What is going on here? The answer comes back in Genesis 1:26: "Then God said, 'Let Us make man in Our image, according to Our likeness; and let them rule over the fish of the sea and over the birds of the sky and over the cattle and over all the earth, and over every creeping thing that creeps on the earth.'" Notice God says, "Let Us make man in Our image"; He is using the plural number—"let Us"—to talk about the nature of the Trinity. There is one God, but in the unity of the Godhead there are three persons, the same in essence but distinct in substance. When God creates in "Our image," He is talking about what is referred to in theology as the *imago dei,* or the "image of God." God is making man in His image. But the image of God is one God in three persons. The Trinity, three in one, is who God is.

What God is saying in Genesis 2:18 is that the image of God is not complete until it is plural in expression. The *imago dei* is fully reflected in plurality.

It is not good that man would be alone. Why? Because man alone does not fully reflect the plurality of the Godhead. So, God creates woman to complement man and make man complete to express fully the image of God.

God could have made us complete individuals in every respect. He could have created us without the need for sleep. However, He decided in His wisdom to create us with a dependence upon sleep. He could have created us without the need for food. However, in His wisdom He created us with the need for nutrition. We need God and we need sleep. We need God and we also need food. We need God and we also need each other. God sometimes chooses to meet our needs through intermediaries.

The visible representation of the image of God is best portrayed in plurality. So what did God establish to fully reflect the image of God? He established two institutions—marriage and the church. In marriage, the two become one flesh (Genesis 2:24). In the church, we are one body in Christ. Significantly, the Scriptures encourage us to comfort one another (2 Corinthians 1:3–4), to "accept one another" (Romans 15:7), and to "love one another" (John 13:34). We are not able to fully reflect the plurality of the Godhead as individuals.

We were not created to be alone. We need each other. How can we harness the power that is found in the body of Christ to corporately reach out to a lost world around us? What are some of the things that we can do to reach out to the community?

GET ORGANIZED

I think that the missing staff position in most churches is "evangelist" (Ephesians 4:11–12). Moyer defines the gift of evangelism as "the special ability to communicate the Gospel to sinners and to equip the saints for evangelism."[1] It appears that the church today has overlooked this vital ministry to the body of Christ. We seem to have relegated the gift of evangelism to proclamational strategies and have neglected its importance to the local church.

Realize that getting the church moving in a corporate witness that would allow opportunities for evangelism requires time. If you are a member of a church or a leader in the church, do not get discouraged; just realize that the people in your church will not change overnight. Be flexible and start with one or two who are interested in evangelism.

Keep prayer central to what is happening! Prayer is the foundation for evangelism. You can have the slickest stuff going; however, if God is not in it, nothing is going to happen. Only God is able to lift that veil and bring about salvation. Keep praying! When you think that you have prayed enough, pray some more! It is amazing what happens when you pray.

Challenge the people in your church to pray for just five unbelievers. Pray that they might have an opportunity to share the Gospel with those five people.

Set an earnest example yourself. Believe it or not, people are watching your example. If you are reading this book, chances are you are already a leader or are training to be a leader in evangelism. I often have pastors call me and ask how to get their congregations going in evangelism. I ask, "What are you personally doing in evangelism right now?" Often the answer is, "Nothing."

"What do you expect?" If you are a leader in your congregation, your people will become just like you over a period of time. If you are not excited about evangelism, then the people in your church will not be excited about evangelism. If you are not setting an earnest example yourself, then your people will follow your lead.

Surround yourself with Christians who are willing to do all they can to help in the work of evangelism and set an atmosphere for evangelism to take place. If there is an atmosphere of excitement and expectation, then people will want to be involved. If there is an atmosphere of failure and discouragement, then people will avoid you like the plague.

Make sure that the leadership team is established. Work with the few that God has given you and go for it! You may want to consider the possibility of establishing some type of small group ministry. A small group ministry will give you the opportunity to work with the leadership team, but it will also provide another vehicle to deliver the Gospel in the months ahead.

THREE OPPORTUNITIES

As you organize, be sure to include three opportunities in any corporate strategy. Of these three opportunities, two are easy to accomplish. The middle opportunity is the toughest to provide. However, do not let this be a discouragement to you; you can easily do two out of three!

First, offer basic skill acquisition opportunities. Equip the congregation on how to share the Gospel. Teach them the basics of the Good News and how to share that Good News with an unbeliever. Choose how you are going to equip your people to present the Gospel, and stick with that presentation. Ground your people in that method. There are a number of products on the market that can help you equip your people and accomplish this task.

Make sure that your people understand the disciple-making process. Try to make the process joyful and free from guilt. And help your people understand the strategy that you are employing to reach out to the community.

Second, offer regular evangelism opportunities. I will return to this topic, but remember that once the individual is trained on how to share the Gospel, provide him or her with a place to plug into an ongoing ministry that is involved in reaching out to the community.

Third, offer special evangelism opportunities. Provide special evangelism events designed to help your people in evangelism. This could be a special movie that includes a clear presentation of the Gospel or a dinner with a special speaker who will present the Gospel. It could be a men's breakfast or a ladies' luncheon that includes a testimony or Gospel presentation. It could be a Valentine's Day banquet for couples with a special message. Such events can help your people share the Gospel with their friends and neighbors. Any of these events may be just the tool that unlocks the door for someone to be able to share the good news of Jesus Christ.

AN EVANGELISM CALENDAR

You may want to think about an evangelism calendar. An evangelism calendar uses the natural events of the year as opportunities to schedule special events at the church. The calendar year works very naturally on a three-trimester time frame. Realizing the three peaks of people's interests and taking advantage of those times will help enhance your outreach into the community. The three peaks are: returning to school (or the job) each fall, celebrating Christmas each winter, and celebrating Easter each spring.

There are cultivation events, sowing events, and harvesting events. Cultivation events are designed to build bridges with unbelievers and cultivate relationships. Examples of cultivation events might be a picnic or a dinner or a baseball game. Any event that has its sole purpose just to build relationships with unbelievers would be categorized as a cultivation event.

A sowing event is where the abundant life is introduced. This could be a marriage seminar where principles of marriage are introduced; however, it is always pointing toward a deeper and more intimate relationship with your spouse through Jesus Christ. It could be a movie on parenting where tips are given, yet there is a hint of the abundant life that is available in Jesus Christ. It could be a seminar on finances that makes the distinction between the temporal and the eternal and encourages people to store up for themselves treasures in heaven. Sowing events give information based on biblical principles, always pointing toward the abundant life in Jesus Christ.

Think through the different types
of events your church [could] host.

Harvesting events are designed to present the Gospel. This could be a men's breakfast that has a special speaker who is prepared to give his testimony on his new life in Christ. It could be a banquet for couples that has a speaker present the Gospel. These are events that are solely designed with the Gospel presentation in mind.

Think through the different types of events your church may want to host. There is an appropriate time for just cultivating relationships.

There is an appropriate time to sow and an appropriate time to harvest. Thinking through the year will help plan your strategy.

Let me give an example. In September, what will occur in a couple of months that provides a natural bridge to the Gospel message? Christmas! If I know that Christmas is coming in December, what can I do in September to enhance my people's outreach? I may choose to have a picnic just to cultivate the ground and build some relationships with the neighborhood. I may choose to have an Octoberfest celebration with the sole purpose of building bridges with people.

As Thanksgiving draws closer, I may choose to sow a few seeds and talk about God's goodness and faithfulness. Or I may choose to host a movie night at the church that informs families and sows a few seeds. I may have an informational seminar for the community to point neighbors toward the source of true life. As Christmas gets closer, I know that I have already cultivated some of the ground, built some relationships, sown a few seeds; now the field may be ripe for the Gospel to be presented.

After Christmas I know that a natural opportunity will occur to share the Gospel about three months into the new year. Easter is coming! So what can I do in January to build relationships with individuals, knowing that I might have the opportunity to share the Gospel down the road? Maybe in January I can plan a cultivation event. Maybe in February I can plan a Valentine's Day banquet for couples that sows a few seeds.

Get the idea? Use the natural calendar events of the year to stimulate evangelism in your congregation.

GET YOUR PEOPLE INVOLVED IN MINISTRY AND SERVICE

Once your people are equipped to be able to share the Gospel, it is imperative to have places of ministry that they might plug into quickly. A wide variety of evangelistic opportunities for your people is desirable. Encourage multiple points of contact for your people.

Here is another basic principle of evangelism. *Evangelism moves forward as God's people get involved in ministry and service.* If I am able to get my people involved in service, and they give themselves away in ministry, evangelism will take care of itself.

Just love people! This can take place a number of different ways. It can happen through educational ministries, including such activities as Vacation Bible School or seminars that deal with marriage, parenting, money, retirement, medical information, leadership, or any number of topics. Other educational ministries might be weekly Bible clubs, home Bible studies, or Sunday school ministries. You may even host some public forums on hot topics that may impact your community, all with the view that you may be able to touch some in your neighborhood with the Gospel.

Your church might also explore ministries to singles or unwed mothers. You might host a ministry to high-school students in the afternoon through some type of sports ministry. Other opportunities exist in a ministry to international students, or the local jails, prisons, children's homes, halfway houses, or hospitals in the area.

Both youth and seniors are . . . asking the same question:
What is life all about?

One ministry that I believe many churches overlook is ministry to the older adults. The church spends a lot of time and resources on youth ministry. I believe that should certainly continue. We program a number of opportunities for our youth, who usually have limited time or money to participate; however, we often do not spend any programming resources on our senior adults, who have both the time and the money to participate.

Both youth and seniors are looking at their lives and asking the same question: What is life all about? Both require a lot of time and patience; what are we doing to minister effectively to that large population segment who are retired?

I encourage churches to think about this vast ministry opportunity. The programming within the two groups is very similar. A church may want to hire a seniors pastor and even a part-time nurse (perhaps a retired professional) to help the people relate to the medical community and deal with medical questions that may arise in this population group. The goal is to be creative and minister to their needs.

Another opportunity that is often overlooked is using various media, including theater. Puppets are a great tool to introduce the Gospel. They are able to get away with things that we are unable to get away with. If I walk into a mall and ask the mall officials if I can stand in the middle of the mall and preach the Gospel, the answer is going to be no. However, if I walk into a mall with a puppet show, amazingly the puppets will be able to say things that I am unable to say. What an opportunity!

ONE CHURCH EXAMPLE

Let me encourage you with an example from one church on the East Coast that has multiple points of contact in the community. This medium-sized church is consciously thinking about ways to get their people involved in reaching out. These suggestions could be applied to any church in the United States, which is exactly the point.

The church has a number of opportunities to reach out. Among their programs:

- A regularly held men's breakfast. The men meet every other month in the fellowship hall. Up to 40 percent of the men who attend the breakfast are not church attenders. Invitation is by card and follow-up.
- A creative monthly program appealing to women's interests. Leaders organize art shows, craft shows, and fashion shows. Occasionally they host a brunch with a special speaker.

- A "coffeehouse" presenting music once a month around tables and candlelight. Those coming enjoy coffee, soft drinks, snacks, and conversation and listen to a featured Christian artist.
- Monthly discussion groups held in strategically located homes. The groups provide an open forum for a lively discussion, and a number of unbelievers attend. The format is casual, typically with questions and answers to generate discussion.
- Several ongoing Bible studies in homes, some church sponsored, some not, which produce not only new converts but also frequent visitors to the church.
- Numerous media outreaches. One is a thriving puppet ministry; a special team of people in the church built their own puppets and stage, and now produce their own plays in-house and present them throughout the community. The church also publishes a bimonthly outreach newspaper featuring apologetics, testimonies, and upcoming events. Musical concerts are also part of their planning. They bring in a top Christian personality or team of professionals and put on a musical happening.
- A spring banquet. This big event features either outstanding entertainers or a musical team along with a quality meal, and it's free for guests; regular attenders pay for their own tickets. This is a major outreach event for them. And each October the church hosts a fall harvest evening to build relationships with people in the community.
- The church's small groups also are individually involved in outreach activities. One group runs a "welcome wagon" for the church. They write letters and even take a small gift to new residents in the community. Another small group is into hosting educational seminars, while another targets their community during Thanksgiving. Other groups specialize in home entertainment, breakfasts, and luncheons.

By the way, the church once hosted a churchwide visitation program; however, they found that their small groups were able to do this ministry better. They stopped the program at the church and moved the responsibility to the small groups.

As you look over this list of what this church is doing, it should be clear that anyone within the church should be able to find a place to plug in. If you trained someone from this church to share the Gospel, he or she should find opportunities to get involved with unbelievers.

Although this church is medium size, with about four hundred in attendance, a small church has just as many opportunities to maximize their effectiveness.[2] In such a church, when someone asks, "What can I do to get involved?" the answer is, "What do you like to do?" Everything, from entertainment and producing to Bible studies, apologetics, and writing, is available for an individual to explore. Plus, if you were unable to find it at the church, I am sure you could start it with the church's blessing and financial backing.

MOVING EVANGELISM FORWARD

Evangelism moves forward as God's people get involved in ministry and service. As people are trained and equipped in evangelism and are involved in regular and consistent contact with unbelievers, evangelism will take place.

How can you be involved in your church? What can you do to stimulate the church in evangelism? What are your gifts and interests that may contribute to the outreach of your church?

We were never designed to be alone. Evangelism is best served as we work together. Send in the herd!

TWELVE:
TELL YOUR STORY!

THE MOST IMPORTANT event in my life happened while driving a car. Let me explain.

When I was a sophomore at the University of Cincinnati, things were going very well. The U.S. Air Force had given me a full scholarship. I owned a car, I owned a sailboat, and I had a private pilot's license. From an outward perspective, things were going just the way things ought to go. I really did not have a care in life.

Then my parents returned from a visit with my older brother. Dan had just completed his tour of duty in Vietnam and was still in the Air Force, stationed in Texas. They announced, "Your brother has changed. Jesus Christ has changed his life."

I was taken aback with shock. This was the time of the "Jesus freak" movement, and all I could think of was that Dan had definitely gone off the deep end and had become a Jesus freak! So, I did the only rational and intelligent thing I could think of at the moment . . . I wrote him off as some kind of nut.

Unfortunately, he was coming home to Ohio that summer for a visit. I did not want to have anything to do with him. In fact, I tried to do everything that I could to avoid him. I think on the one hand I was afraid of him, but I also thought that if I talked with him, *my* life might change as well. And that was scary. Because I was much too cool for that! In my mind, this "Christian" thing (whatever that is) might change my style. *After all,* I reasoned, *I do not need this Jesus.*

When my brother came home, I was unable to avoid him. He followed me everywhere, talking about Jesus. But the conversation that changed my life happened as I was driving across town to get some parts for my sailboat. Dan crawled into my car and began to talk to me about what had transpired in his life. I don't remember his exact words, but I do remember that there were a couple of important points.

He talked about how he had depended for so long on his own abilities and talents to be able to make it through life. And he had been very successful at it. "But through it all," Dan said, "there was still an emptiness in my life."

My brother went on to tell me that God is a God of love. "He really wants to have a loving relationship with us," Dan said, quoting John 3:16. "But God is also a God of perfection. His absolute moral perfection is the standard upon which that relationship is based." Listening to Dan, I knew that I was less than perfect.

"I fall short of God's standard of perfection; you fall short of His standard. The Bible calls falling short of God's perfection sin" (Romans 3:23). Then my brother explained that the wages of my imperfection—the wages of my sin—was death (Romans 6:23). Death is what I have earned.

Now that's bad news. But my brother also shared with me some good news.

The good news is Christ died in my place. "Jesus Christ died for you," Dan said. God substituted Christ's perfection for my imperfection through His death on the cross, burial, and resurrection (Romans 5:8). Jesus Christ died in my place making a relationship with God possible.

"All you need to do is believe!" Dan said.

Believe means to trust Jesus Christ to forgive my sins and bring me into a right relationship with God (Romans 4:5), he explained. "Trust in Christ's perfection and payment that He made on your behalf. That's the only way to a right relationship with God, Doug. Believing involves not only understanding and agreeing with the facts that Christ died for you and arose from the dead; it also involves transferring your trust from your own efforts to make yourself acceptable to God, to what Jesus Christ has already accomplished on the Cross."

I made that decision while I was stopped at a traffic light on Eastern Avenue in Cincinnati, Ohio, with my brother next to me in the passenger seat. It was there that I transferred my trust to Jesus Christ.

That decision changed my life. Life since that moment in my green Oldsmobile convertible has been good. Oh, I still have problems. I still have frustrations. However, since that moment my perspective on life has changed. I am no longer striving to just please myself. That emptiness, the void, the vacuum in my heart is no longer there. The vacuum has been filled with the inexhaustible One, Jesus Christ.

WHAT'S YOUR STORY?

The most powerful tool that you have to share the Gospel is your evangelistic personal testimony. Notice that I said, "The most powerful tool." I put it that forcefully because in today's culture I am convinced that if we are able to tell our story effectively, we can reach many people. Unfortunately, our story of how we came to place our trust in Christ is one of the most misunderstood and misused tools around. The reason for that is probably due to the way that we normally hear testimonies presented.

Normally we hear testimonies on Sunday evening or during a midweek service that is designed to encourage or edify believers. These services are usually more casual in nature, so a testimony fits in well. Typically we will hear about a radically changed life—a story of desperation and rescue from sin that shocks and yet encourages the believers present that there is still a God who cares and hears the cries of sinners.

It's as if we find the biggest and worst dude to tell his desperation story. He stands up and says, "I was bad. I was mean. I was awful. But . . . God changed my life! I am a new person all over! I was washed in the blood and God began His sanctifying work in my life."

> An evangelistic personal testimony is a clear statement of your conversion with a Gospel presentation woven in.

As believers, we listen to that story and are encouraged. We see that sorry individual and reason that if God was able to change his life, then there is hope for our lives as well. That testimony is designed primarily to encourage believers in their spiritual life. That is *not* the type of testimony that I am talking about in this chapter.

I am talking about an evangelistic personal testimony that is designed primarily for *unbelievers*. An evangelistic personal testimony is not an insider's story for insiders, and it does not use exclusively Christian terms. An evangelistic personal testimony is a clear statement of your conversion with a Gospel presentation woven in, so that an unbeliever can understand the Gospel and respond.

Maybe some who are reading these words came to place their trust in Christ at a very early age. It would be interesting to know how many of those who came to place their trust in Christ at an early age somehow feel that their story is in some way inferior to those radically changed life scenarios that are normally presented.

Whatever your story, you have a powerful tool to share the Gospel. Pagans normally do not pursue holiness.

One of my students, who I'll call Jim, once told classmates about the impact of his undramatic conversion. He had trusted Christ before the age of six, had married the girl of his dreams and her testimony was the same as his, almost to the year. They were both frustrated over their testimony and "wished we had one of those radically saved testimonies that really turn heads and win converts. But neither of us had been neglected, molested, abused, raped, addicted, in prison, wanted, or adulterous, and even if we had it would have been when we were Christians. What a bum deal."

He had become involved in a prison ministry. After a few visits to the prison, Jim wished that he had some experience that would "grant me the right to share" with these men of such desperate pasts. Instead he would rely upon other stories and keep the conversation clear of himself.

That was until one day when two inmates suddenly asked him, "Well, what about you?"

"What do you mean?" he responded. "What about me about what?"

"What about you with this Jesus stuff?" they asked.

So he took a breath and shared his story. From stories on the bed told by his father to where he was right then.

They both trusted Christ in their cells that night. The next time Jim saw them he asked them what had happened. This is what they said. "You came from a family that had everything. Your parents were married, you lived in a great house, and you had a dad that loved you enough to read you stories. You had everything! Yet you still felt like you needed Jesus, and that blew us away because we always figured that the only people that ever turned to Jesus were those that were just hoping for a way out or for a quick fix or something like that. And then you said that you had been walking with Jesus for all these years and you're still doing this deal!

"We knew that if you started like that and have been living with Him all this time and you are here today still walking with the Lord, then He must be real!"

Their response changed his thinking about testimonies. Today he presents his testimony every chance he gets because he realizes that no matter what one's past has been, his personal testimony is a valuable tool. People do not normally pursue holiness.

While my testimony will revolve around a "rescue from sin" scenario, your testimony, if you trusted Christ at a young age, will revolve around a "preservation from sin" scenario. Either way, the world does not get it!

If you trusted Christ at an early age, you may want to consider starting your story with the present and then going back to how you came to this place in your life. Nobody says that an evangelistic testimony has to start when you were born.

People can identify with a testimony. An evangelistic personal testimony has authority in it (John 9:25). In fact, your testimony is a very powerful tool, especially against Satan (Revelation 12:10–11).

A STEP-BY-STEP PROCESS OF PREPARING YOUR TESTIMONY

Preparing your evangelistic personal testimony is as easy as ABC.[1] *First,* ask *the Holy Spirit to guide the selection and preparation of the words you speak.* One would not think of going into the pulpit or teaching situation without bathing the message in prayer, and this is no exception.

Decide on whether you will use a theme in your testimony. Your theme may revolve around unrealistic expectations, religion versus a relationship with Jesus Christ, rituals, acceptance, being a good person or doing the right things, appearances, applause, the American dream, being a people pleaser, or fighting old ghosts in your life. A theme can bring interest and identity to your testimony.

Select an interesting introduction. Be creative! Or you may choose to simply say something like, "I would like to share something with you that has been very meaningful to me." Be yourself, but try to grab the listener's attention.

Second, be brief *and to the point about your past.* Share something about life before knowing Christ. Make it relevant and thought provoking. Give sufficient detail so that people can see you are a real person. However, watch out, because people are able to quickly get the idea about your past, and it is usually unnecessary to go into a lot of detail.

Identify the root of the problem (sin) and not so much the fruit of the problem. An event or tendency that you have that happened in the past may be the root of the problem, while all of the other events surrounding it might be the fruit of that basic problem. A blow-by-blow description of all of the surrounding events and the specifics of those events is often inappropriate.

Often in testimonies that are designed for believers the story revolves around how Jesus made life better. No doubt that is true. But the issue to an unbeliever is sin and what Jesus did to pay that debt and restore the relationship sin had broken. Those are key elements in a Gospel presentation.

Make a comment about how you came to know Christ. What were you thinking? What were you feeling? What was going on in your life that caused you to be open to the Gospel? What led you to make the decision to trust Christ?

Part of being brief is to share the basics of the Good News. Be brief and specific about how you came to know Jesus Christ as your personal Savior. How specifically did you place your trust in Him? The person listening to your story should be able to walk away from their time with you and understand the basics of the Good News. Even if he does not place his trust in Christ right then, he should know how that takes place. Share how it happened for you.

As you give the basics, avoid Christian jargon. Translate your Christian words so that an unbeliever can understand them. Avoid glittering generalities that are unbelievable.

Avoid talking about denominations and using Christian terms. While a particular denomination or group may have had an impact in your life, it is probably best to leave out the name of that organization or group. The reason is that the person listening may not have the same feelings about that group that you have, even if he or she is familiar with that group. You may have great feelings about a particular organization; however, your listener may not share those feelings. Why introduce another issue? You may just want to say that you got involved with a group on campus. Or that you decided to go to a church where the Bible was taught.

> *Ask* the Holy Spirit to guide,
> *be brief,* and *center* on Christ.

Make a comment about what is happening in your life right now. Focus on the now of your experience with Jesus Christ. Be brief and real about your present walk with Christ. Include how Christ is meeting your needs and the hope that you have for the future. Include what God is doing now in your walk with Him and how He is changing your life right now. Talk about your struggles as well as your victories. But, once again, be careful to avoid "wonderful" superlatives.

This section might also include a closing Scripture passage that has been meaningful to you. Be sure to keep your testimony fresh and up-to-date.

Third, center *on Christ,* not yourself. You obviously must talk about yourself because it is your testimony. However, the person that you desire to elevate and hold out to the lost world is Jesus Christ, not yourself. Keep Jesus Christ as the focal point of everything that has happened.

It's as simple as ABC: *Ask* the Holy Spirit to guide, *be brief,* and *center* on Christ.

At the conclusion of your testimony, you may want to continue with a few questions. "Has everything that I have said been clear to you?" is a good question to see whether the listener has comprehended everything that you have said. "Have you ever placed your trust in Jesus Christ?" "Would you like to place your trust in Jesus Christ right now?"

WHEN YOUR TESTIMONY
IS MOST EFFECTIVE

What are some of the situations where your testimony is most effective? When you stop to think about it, *your testimony is most effective in any casual situation.*

When do you normally hear testimonies in church? Typically you hear testimonies on Sunday evening or during a midweek service. Why? You hear them at those services because they are more casual.

You may also hear them at breakfast presentations, youth gatherings, retreats, and campfire presentations. All of these places have one common element—they are all casual settings.

Testimonies work best when the setting is informal. One of the main problems that we have in sharing the Gospel is making the transition from casual and informal small talk to the topic of the Gospel. One of the reasons that this transition is so difficult is that we are trying to take a casual conversation and transition to a formal presentation.

All the presentations that we learn to share the Gospel are formal presentations. When using a tract you even have a visual aid to your presentation in the form of pictures and charts. It is like having your own flip chart or overhead presentation in your pocket. Making the transition from informal chitchat to a formal presentation is extremely difficult.

The beauty of an evangelistic testimony, in contrast, is that it keeps the conversation in the informal. The conversation remains casual. "Let me tell you my story" is very natural. One benefit of an evangelistic testimony is that it is very easy to identify with a testimony, especially if you are able to communicate your feelings and thoughts during your journey.

USING YOUR TESTIMONY WITH CULTS

Let me add a word here about cults. Over the years, most Christians have been visited by one or more cults. They come to the door, and you try to find some convenient excuse not to talk with them. If you do talk with them, at the end you feel that you were playing some type of verbal volleyball with them and nothing was accomplished.

Maybe you have become a little tired of that, so you have looked for some type of seminar to help you dialogue with these people. The problem is that even after the seminar most of us can't remember what we're supposed to say. From the time of the seminar to the time that they knock on our doors we have forgotten exactly what we are supposed to say and those Scriptures that can corner our opponent.

Perhaps you have a mind that is able to remember all of that stuff. If you do, praise God, we need you! But most Christians can't remember all of those techniques as well. In fact, I would bet that most of the people in our churches are just like us and can't remember that stuff either.

Even if I was able to train the church to be able to deal with every cult that comes to the door, I would not be able to adequately train my family. My family does not have a theological education; what hope do they have, and what can I do to help prepare them for the inevitable visit?

The best way that I have found for my family to be able to share the Gospel with cult members is to present their evangelistic personal testimony.

Usually when a cult comes to your door there is a "big guy" mentor and a "little guy" learner. The big guy is training the little guy and is normally doing all of the talking. Here's what I do, and I recommend the approach to you. I will wait for the initial opening to subside and then offer to share with them what has happened in my life. I talk about how Jesus Christ died for my sins and arose from the dead. I talk about how He is coming back. I talk about how a *personal relationship with Jesus Christ changed my life.* And then I ask them if there is anything keeping them from placing their trust in Jesus Christ.

Typically they look at me as if I was some type of alien creature, terminate the conversation, and begin to walk down our front walkway. About halfway down the walkway the big guy will turn to the little guy and say, "He is a nut." That is my clue to pray for them. *You see, they are not the enemy; they are deceived by the Enemy.* My prayer is that maybe over time enough Christians will be able to share their testimony with them so that the little guy might be moved to reconsider his position. I really do not think that the big guy is going to change apart from a miraculous work of the Lord, but maybe the little guy will.

Once I started using this technique to share with cult members, the cult members at my door no longer frightened me. I knew what I was going to say. I was able to loosen up and feel confident in the conversation. And so can you.

USING YOUR TESTIMONY IN THIS CULTURE

Today's culture has become more and more diversified, both racially and in their belief systems. Our society has become more biblically illiterate, and "tolerance" has become a key word.

The key phrases that we hear today are "whatever," "everything is relative," and "that's all right for you." Experience has become the final authority in life. There is no such thing as objective truth or moral absolutes. *Tolerance* today means all things are right and people should accept all viewpoints.

In such a culture, where Bible knowledge is limited and all viewpoints seem accepted, how in the world can we present the Gospel? The best tool that you have to present the Gospel to this culture is your evangelistic personal testimony. The challenge is to be authentic and relevant. Two questions that the society today is asking are, "Is he real?" and "Does it work?"

I know a pastor who ministers in a very difficult place; in fact, it is probably one of the more difficult places in the country. In his community witchcraft and the occult are running rampant. Homosexuality is embraced without any shame. As he drove me down the main street of his community there were a number of different styles of dress and makeup. Yet he is leading people to Christ on a regular basis!

> "Just listen to them
> and love them."

"How do you do it?" I asked. His response was a classic. He said, "First, it took me two years to get over my own stuff. The body piercing, the wild hair, the makeup, all of these things are just a defense mechanism to keep people away. It took me two years to begin to look at the person rather than the wild getup. Then I just listen to them and love them."

"Listen to them and love them." That is true wisdom in any culture. That is what it is all about, isn't it? This pastor then explained that as soon as he just sat down with them and listened to their stories and what was important to them, it was easy to begin to show how God's story intersected their stories. In fact, he said that his church had just started a millennial generation service. I asked him what a millennial service was, and with a sly smile on his face he answered, "Oh, it is just a contemporary service with more candles."

My friend had found a way to reach out to his community. However, it was not any different than all of us reaching out to our own communities. Listen to them and love them.

Because there is more biblical illiteracy in our culture, you cannot assume that everyone whom you talk with understands the true nature of God. You may need to start with God. Center on the Bible and Jesus Christ. Believe it or not, they really do want to know what the Bible has to say on the subject of life.

Tell your story. Your story is relevant. It can be shared in a casual and nonthreatening way. And your story to this generation is authoritative. Your experience has power. It is real and it is authentic.

When someone asks me, "How do I share the Gospel with the postmodern?" the answer is twofold. First, find out where they are. Listen to their stories and find out where you might need to begin. Second, tell them your story. Your evangelistic personal testimony is powerful. Don't be afraid to use it.

The most powerful tool that you have at your disposal to share the Gospel is your evangelistic personal testimony. Keep working on it and keep it up-to-date.

THIRTEEN:
A NATURAL EXTENSION OF YOU AND YOUR MINISTRY

ONE AFTERNOON DURING my weekly visits as a hospital chaplain, I met a bedridden lady who was approximately ten years older than I. Although she was slight, she rested in a bright and cheery room with cards and flowers nearby from those concerned for her.

We had a wonderful talk. But the thing that I remember the most about this visit was not the lady, but what happened.

I was talking, but my mind soon slipped off to thinking of something else. My mind had clicked into another train of thought: *Here I am sharing the Gospel with this lady, and I do not remember how I got here!*

All this happened naturally. Normally I would go into a room and immediately begin to think about how I might turn the conversation around to spiritual things. *How can I make the transition from small talk to talking about the significant matters of Jesus Christ and eternal life?*

There I was talking about the Gospel, and I did not know how I got there! I do not remember how I made the transition. It just happened naturally. I walked out of that room praising God. The Gospel had become at that moment a natural extension of me. Talking about the Gospel to that lady was natural and not forced.

Now I must confess that I still have times when I think about how to make a transition with a person. However, the experience of finding myself sharing the Gospel without any clue of how I made the transition to spiritual things has become more a reality in my life.

At this moment, sharing the Gospel for you may be a burden; you are always consciously thinking about how to make the transition from the typical topics of the day to spiritual things. Let me encourage you: You can get to a place where the Gospel will be a natural part of your lifestyle, an extension of who you are.

You may be asking yourself, *But how do I get to that place? Where do I begin?* Five principles can help as you seek to make evangelism part of your lifestyle.

IT ALL STARTS WITH PRAYER

First, all evangelism starts with prayer. C. H. Spurgeon, evangelist and minister of the Metropolitan Tabernacle in London, wrote,

> The soul winner must be a master of the art of prayer. You cannot bring souls to God if you go not to God yourself. You must get your battle ax and your weapons of war from the armory of sacred communication with Christ. If you are much alone with Jesus, you will catch His Spirit. You will be fired with the flame that burned in His breast and consumed His life. You will weep with the tears that fell upon Jerusalem when He saw it perishing. If you cannot speak as eloquently as He did, yet shall there be about what you say somewhat of the same power which in Him thrilled the hearts and awoke the consciences of men.[1]

Prayer gets you in tune with the Father's heart. It helps you to see people the way God sees people. When we are able to love people the way God loves people, our message will come across in love and genuine compassion. You cannot manufacture Christlike love in the flesh. You can only love in the Spirit. Prayer helps to bring that about.

Lewis Sperry Chafer, founder of Dallas Theological Seminary, wrote, "When a soul has received the redemption which is in Christ and is saved, that one is then privileged to suffer with Christ in a compassion for the lost—being prompted, in some measure, by the same divine vision and love, through the presence and power of the indwelling Spirit."[2]

What should we pray about? *First, pray for opportunity* (Colossians 4:3). Paul talks about the "door" of opportunity being opened to him in 1 Corinthians 16:9 and 2 Corinthians 2:12. Pray that God might open that door of opportunity for you. Unless the Holy Spirit opens that door, the Gospel will stay at the doorstep.

Chafer wrote, "Intercessory prayer is the first and most important service. As has been stated, the divine order is to talk to God about men, until the door is definitely open to talk to men about God."[3]

Second, pray for your effectiveness. Second Thessalonians 3:1 reads, "Finally, brothers, pray for us that the message of the Lord may spread rapidly and be honored, just as it was with you" (NIV). Pray that the Gospel might have free rein in the unbeliever's life.

Third, pray for the unbeliever. Pray specifically for the lost person. First Timothy 2:1 reads, "I urge that entreaties and prayers, petitions and thanksgivings, be made on behalf of all men." Pray that God would lift that veil from their eyes that they might clearly hear the words of the Gospel.

"Fundamentally, then, the personal element in true soul-winning work is more a service of pleading *for* souls than a service of pleading *with* souls. It is talking with God about men from a clean heart and in the power of the Spirit, rather than talking to men about God."[4]

Who are the unbelievers you know that you are praying for now, asking God to prepare for hearing the Gospel? Evangelism is more spiritual than it is methodological. We need to constantly be before the Lord acknowledging our dependence upon Him and asking for His strength and boldness. I need to be asking God to open the door of opportunity and do a mighty work in the unbeliever's life.

BE OBEDIENT

Second, when everything is said and done, it really comes down to making a choice to be obedient to God's Word and get involved in evangelism. I need to make a decision to develop an evangelistic lifestyle.

Without making that decision, evangelism will be erratic. It will come and go based upon our emotions at that moment and not as a result of our walk with the Spirit. Often evangelism is the result of some type of program or emotional experience. There is nothing wrong with programs or experience; however, if that is the only thing that motivates your evangelistic ministry, then evangelism will be very erratic. If you have already decided that evangelism is part of your lifestyle, then you are always alert to the opportunities.

The person who has been praying for opportunities is alert to what God might be doing in somebody's life and eager to play a part. The person who has already decided what is going to happen in a given situation is more sensitive to what the Holy Spirit might be doing.

> Passion is released through obedience [and]
> can be further developed through obedience.

Without making a decision to develop an evangelistic lifestyle, a major ingredient in your spiritual life is lost. You were built to have an impact on the world. If there is not some type of outreach going on in your life, then a major part of your spiritual life is anemic.

Maybe you are saying right now, "You know, I understand what you are saying, but I just don't feel anything." Remember, obedience leads to passion. Recall from chapter 5 the principle found in Matthew 28:19–20: Our doubts will be dispelled through obedience to God's command. When the disciples came to meet our Lord on the mountain, some worshipped and some were doubtful. Jesus knew that they had doubts; however, He did not talk about their doubts. He said, "Do this." Gideon in Judges 6–7 is another good example of one whose doubts were dispelled through obedience. Our doubts are diminished and often disappear as we become obedient to God's Word.

However, the principle goes further than that. Passion can be further developed through obedience. Because of the ministry of the Holy Spirit, there is a natural passion for evangelism in your life. As you become obedient to God's Word and take it by faith, passion is developed.

There is a natural ingrown passion and a developed passion. Ingrown passion is released through obedience. Developed passion can be further developed through obedience. I know some passionate fishermen. They would rather be on the lake attacking fish than anywhere else. I do not have that same passion for fishing. Was their passion for bass fishing ingrown or developed? I believe that it was developed. They were not born with a passion for bass fishing. Due to some influence in their life, maybe a father, grandfather, or friend, they were introduced to the thrill of bass fishing. Their passion was developed.

With evangelism, because of the indwelling of the Holy Spirit, you already have a passion for evangelism. However, that passion can be further developed and nurtured through obedience.

Recognize that evangelism is for you. Those commands in Scripture are for you, not someone else. Be prepared (1 Peter 3:15) and be flexible in evangelism (1 Corinthians 9:19).

Recognize that you have a unique sphere in evangelism. Wherever you live, work, or play, the people that you meet are within your sphere of influence. You will meet people that I will never meet. Similarly, I will meet and come in contact with people that you will never see. I need to be praying for those folks that are within my sphere.

Remember that how we live serves as a foundation for evangelism and not as a substitute. Christianity is enshrined in the life, but it is proclaimed by the lips. I need to be ready and open to present the Good News to those with whom I come in contact.

Maintain or renew your commitment to the church. An evangelistic lifestyle begins with the local church. As brothers and sisters encourage you, that love will spill out into a lost world. Plus, when those you evangelize become Christians, the first people they will come in contact with are people in the church. So be involved with the body of Christ.

Remember that an evangelistic lifestyle is person centered and not program centered. Our ministry to people needs to be in connection with the ordinary needs of life and meeting those needs.

HAVE A CLEAR OUTLINE
OF THE GOSPEL IN MIND

Beyond prayer and obedience is a third principle for developing an evangelistic lifestyle, where evangelism becomes a natural extension of your life: Have a clear presentation of the Gospel in mind. Without a clear Gospel, you will freeze up and be so worried about what you are going to say next that you forget to be real. With a clear outline in mind, you have the foundation to be able to flex with the particulars of each situation.

The Gospel is simple enough for my four-year-old child to understand! We do not have to make it difficult if the Holy Spirit is in it. When my kids came to trust Christ, it was pretty simple. They knew that they were sinful. They knew that Jesus took the penalty for their sin. And they put their trust in Him as the only way to be acceptable to God.

All of the issues that we seem to wrestle with today in our theological circles were not relevant to my kids. Did my children know anything about the hypostatic union (the union of human and divine natures in Jesus Christ)? No, even though that concept is crucial to understanding who Jesus Christ is, it was irrelevant to my kids. What did they know about the *kenosis* (the self-emptying of Christ)?[4] Nothing. Even though that is essential to what was going on at the Cross, they could care less. They were just concerned about coming to Jesus.

What are we required to introduce? What topics do we need to make sure that they understand? *The Gospel message is "Christ died for my sin and arose from the dead."* We might be tempted to introduce a number of topics that may not be relevant. Some want to talk about the Bible. Some want to emphasize God's love. Some want to talk about the deity of Christ. All of those are important; however, what is really essential?

The wonderful nature of the Gospel is that it is able to meet people where they are. We do not know exactly what the thief on the cross understood as Jesus told him, "Truly I say to you, today you shall be with Me in Paradise" (Luke 23:43). What was actually communicated when the Philippian jailer asked, "'Sirs, what must I do to be saved?' They [Paul and Silas] said, 'Believe in the Lord Jesus, and you will be saved, you and your household'" (Acts 16:30–31). Since neither Jesus nor Paul felt compelled to explain all of the theological details concerning the deity of Christ, or the inerrancy of Scripture or the vastness of God's love, neither should we feel compelled to consider these topics essential to introduce.

In today's culture, many unbelievers may be wrestling with different topics. One may be wrestling with the whole concept of God. Another may be wrestling with the deity of Jesus Christ. Maybe the issue of the Bible being God's Word is a stumbling block to someone else. Still another may not have an understanding of sin; or maybe there is some other issue on her mind.

It may be appropriate at some time to dialogue about those issues; however, to presuppose what an unbeliever is wrestling with is inappropriate. I do not know where an individual unbeliever is in his spiritual journey. You and I do not know what he has been exposed to and what he has been taught. We do not know whether he has a biblical background or not. To make an assumption either way would be inappropriate.

Because America is becoming more and more biblically illiterate, we must be careful to not presuppose a certain level of biblical understanding in our presentations of the Gospel. We may or may not be right. Remember, *a good Gospel presentation is a conversation and not a sermon.*

THREE ESSENTIALS IN A GOSPEL OUTLINE

For that presentation, have a clear outline of the Gospel in mind. A good outline gives you the confidence that you need to know what ultimately needs to be presented—and it helps the conversation be a conversation and not a formal presentation. When you know where you are going, you can engage in a dialogue instead of a sermon.

Keep the outline simple. Be faithful to communicate the Gospel in the power of the Holy Spirit and leave the results to God. My presentation follows the three main parts of the Gospel: sin, substitutionary atonement, and faith.

First, I want to talk about sin. I read Romans 3:23 and point out that "all have sinned." That includes me. I then try to ask something like, "If I were to ask you if you were a sinner, what would you say?" Usually the person will admit that he is a sinner. When the person does this, it gives me the opportunity to ask, "What would you say sin is?" I stress that sin means "falling short" of God's perfection. But sin is not only what we do; it is also who we are. We not only break God's commands, but we were born sinful. Because one sinned (Adam), we all have sinned (Romans 5:12).

I add an illustration here about falling short. We all fall short of God's perfection. "Suppose I were to challenge you to swim from California to Hawaii," I sometimes say. "I might swim a little farther than you, or you might swim a little farther than me, but we would both fall short of making it to Hawaii. Whether we both try to throw a rock to hit the North Pole, or whether we both try to swim from California to Hawaii, we all fall short of the target. God's target is perfection, and we all fall short."

I then read Romans 6:23 and point out that due to our sin, we have all earned death. There is physical death and spiritual death (spiritual separation from God). The Bible says that due to our sin we have all earned spiritual separation from God. I will ask, "What do you think spiritual separation from God means?" To put the concept of spiritual separation from God very abruptly, it means hell.

If I get to sin and the listener has no knowledge of what I am talking about, I will go back and fill in some of the blanks. I may need to talk more about sin if the unbeliever has no clue about what I am saying.

Second, I talk about substitutionary atonement. I read Romans 5:8 and ask another series of questions. "According to our last verse, due to our sin what did we earn?"

"Death."

"Right. What does this verse say that Christ did?"

"He died for our sins."

"Right again. What do you think that means?"

I explain that Christ died in our place. He took that which was causing our death and placed it upon Himself and died for us. I may use any number of illustrations here to explain the point—from someone taking the penalty that I have earned, to someone taking my terminal illness on himself to die in my place. "Suppose that I was dying of cancer," I might say. "If someone volunteered to take my cancer out of my body and place it into himself, what would happen to him? He would die instead of me. I would live. He would die. Jesus came and took the penalty that we deserve for sin, placed it upon Himself, and died in my place. He died for my sins and arose from the dead. His resurrection proved that His substitutionary death was an acceptable sacrifice to God."

Maybe as I talk about substitutionary atonement, the person has some questions about the deity of Jesus Christ. In that case I could go back and talk about Jesus' deity (citing, for example, John 1:1 and 10:30).

If the person remains unclear about the Resurrection, I could deal with the issue (looking at portions of 1 Corinthians 15:1–28).

Then I will review. "Let's review. First, we are sinners. The wages of sin is death. But, Christ died for our sins and arose from the dead. He died in our place. He took our sins upon Himself and He died for you." I am really sensitive to the work of the Holy Spirit here, because you can sense whether the unbeliever is tracking with you.

Third, I talk about faith. I will read either Ephesians 2:8–9 or Romans 4:4–5, depending upon the person that I am talking to and the conversation up to this point. The point I make is that works cannot save. Only faith in Christ can save. Faith means to trust Christ and Him alone as the only way to be reconciled to a holy God. Faith not only means believing the facts, but means total trust, depending upon Christ alone for forgiveness of our sins.

I follow up that point with an illustration. I might talk about the chair that he is sitting on. I might talk about how we demonstrate total trust when we fly on an airplane. "When I fly on an airplane, I do not check to see if the aircraft is up-to-date on its airworthiness certificate. I do not check to see the pilot's medical certificate and make sure that she has a commercial pilot's license with the appropriate ratings. I walk on the aircraft, sit down, and trust that everything is in order. I have trusted my life to that airplane and pilot. Placing your trust in Jesus Christ is transferring your trust from your own efforts to save you to what Jesus Christ accomplished on the cross."

The determination of what topics
to address rests with the listener, not you.

After illustrating the point, I will ask, "Would you like to trust Christ right now?" If the person says yes, I will ask him if he would like to express to God in prayer that desire. "Prayer does not save anyone," I explain. "It merely is expressing to God your trust in Christ and Christ alone as the only way to be reconciled to Him." If he is still tracking with me I will lead the new believer in prayer. The prayer is nothing magical, but merely acknowledges that one is a sinner. The person thanks God that Christ died on the cross for his or her sins and arose from the dead. And the person can express faith and trust in Christ and Him alone for the forgiveness of all sins.

Remember that this is a dialogue. Faith may be a stumbling block to the unbeliever, so if that is the case, pause and talk a little more about faith. The determination of what topics to address rests with the listener, not you.

A good presentation to use and commit to memory is the "Good News–Bad News"[6] presentation of the Gospel that is a cornerstone of the ministry of EvanTell. Whatever presentation you choose, memorize the main points until you feel comfortable with it.

The presentation that you choose becomes a framework for your discussion with the unbeliever. Be alert to his needs; do not force your hobbyhorse on him. Let him raise the issues that need to be raised in his life. Be sensitive to the Holy Spirit. Let Him work. Remember that you are just a tool that He is able to use. He is able to use a number of tools, and by the grace of God, you happen to be the tool that He is choosing to use right now.

WALK IN THE SPIRIT

Fourth, focus on pure motives. I do not intentionally plan for evangelism. If I am walking with the Spirit and *just love people,* evangelism takes care of itself. I am always aware of evangelism, and I am sensitive for evangelism to take place; however, I am not consciously planning to make a transition to spiritual things.

That is a pretty wild concept, isn't it? I want to see people the way that Christ sees people. I want to love people the way that Christ loves

181

people. I cannot manufacture Christ's love in the flesh. That type of love can only come from the Spirit.

We need to be walking with the Spirit for such love to be manifested in us.

Sometimes in evangelism we bring our own personal agendas into the conversation with an unbeliever. Focus on the unbeliever's needs and not your needs. This has everything to do with the spiritual life and walking in the Spirit.

Recognize that you cannot do evangelism in your own power. The first thing that needs to happen is to die to self, according to Romans 6:1–11. The passage teaches that "our old self was crucified with Him . . . that we would no longer be slaves to sin" (v. 6). We are to "consider [ourselves] to be dead to sin, but alive to God in Christ Jesus" (v. 11).

How do we do that? As soon as you ask that question, you have already asked the wrong question. It is not a question of how we do it; it is a question of faith and trust in Jesus Christ. If there is a command in Scripture, we are to obey. If there is a statement of fact in Scripture, we are to believe. Believe it to be true, consider it so, and stand on it. Consider yourself dead to sin because God said it was true.

Offer yourself to God (vv. 12–13). Behavior must follow belief. Offer yourself to God as an instrument of righteousness instead of as an instrument of sin. Renew your mind to line up with God's truth (12:1–2).

As you walk in the Spirit, you become more in tune with God's heart for the world and the prompting of the Spirit in people's lives. This is essential for evangelism to become an extension of your life.

GIVE YOURSELF AWAY IN MINISTRY

Fifth, if you would like evangelism to be a natural extension of your life, focus on giving yourself away in ministry and service. One of the paradoxes of ministry is that if you focus on evangelism, it will be a burden to you. It will be a heavy weight to your soul. You will feel guilty and defeated. However, if you focus on just loving people and giving yourself away in ministry and service, evangelism will take care of itself.

I return to a question that I raised earlier, "What is it that you like to do?" As you get involved in ministry and service in areas that you enjoy, evangelism will naturally take care of itself. As you walk in the Spirit, you can't help but tell everyone about the Savior. Chafer wrote,

> Above all, the personal worker must be wholly dependent upon the leading of the Spirit. He should be as prepared to do the unusual thing as the usual. If really prepared for service, his ear will be open to God concerning every person he may chance to meet, but he will not assume to force a decision without divine direction. With the great commission to preach the gospel to every creature, it may usually be assumed that God would have us speak to men, with all earnestness, unless otherwise led by the Spirit.[7]

Yes, an evangelistic lifestyle can become a natural extension of your life. It has everything to do with your relationship with Jesus Christ. It starts with prayer and continues with obedience and having a clear presentation of the Gospel message in mind. Keep walking in the Spirit and give yourself away in ministry and service. Allow the Spirit to work through you, and evangelism will become a natural extension.

FOURTEEN:
ANSWERING QUESTIONS

THE WELL-DRESSED person next to me was on the same flight to Dallas, and we soon struck up a conversation and talked about a number of different topics. I learned that he actually worked for the federal government and was traveling to Washington, D.C., for the week. He was originally from India and had married an American girl.

Finally he asked me what I did for a living, and I told him that I taught at a seminary. After the initial confusion about a seminary, he confessed that he was really having a difficult time coming to grips with "this concept of God." I asked him what he meant, and he said that he grew up Hindu and married a Roman Catholic. The whole concept of one God was beyond his comprehension.

We had a wonderful conversation about God. I never even got around to the Gospel, because that was not where he was. He was still wrestling with the concept of one supreme God. However, I did challenge him with the Resurrection, which is my default mode when it comes to these types of conversations. I stated, "If you can disprove the Resurrection, you have me. After all, Paul states, 'If there is no resurrection of the dead, then not even Christ has been raised. And if

Christ has not been raised, our preaching is useless and so is your faith. . . . If Christ has not been raised, your faith is futile; you are still in your sins'" (1 Corinthians 15:13–14, 17 NIV).

I suggested that he read a book entitled *Who Moved the Stone?* by Frank Morison.[1] The man lit up! He said, "I think that I have that book!" He reached into his briefcase and pulled out a copy of Morison's book!

I asked him what in the world he was doing with a copy of that book. He responded that there were two Christian men in his office back in Los Angeles, and they had been talking to him about these same topics for quite a long time. On Friday, knowing that he would be in Washington, D.C., for a week, they had given him a copy of Morison's book in hope that he might read it while he was away.

"Do you think I should read it?" he asked.

"Absolutely!" I replied.

I got off that plane rejoicing. I had been used of God in a way that I didn't anticipate. I was now praying that those two brothers back in L. A. would have the privilege of seeing that man come to trust Christ.

Even though I did not have the opportunity to share the Gospel with that man, I was used by God to answer some of his questions and objections. That man was still lost when he got off the airplane; however, answering his questions was a bridge for someone to share the Gospel.

When I talk about answering questions I am referring to questions regarding the Christian faith. A defense of the Christian faith is called an "apologetic." The word comes from the Greek word meaning a verbal defense, an answer, or a reply. An apologetic is a presentation of the reasons why we believe what we believe.

Before we look at the seventh and final principle of an evangelistic life, let's consider the role of apologetics in helping the unbeliever come to faith. We may be at principle six—actually presenting the Gospel by natural means through acts of service that include a Gospel presentation. We may be sharing our personal testimony and succeeding in making evangelism a natural extension of our lifestyle. Yet some genuine seekers may seem unready to commit, stumbling over questions. They seem unable to listen to or understand the Gospel. They cannot apprehend the Gospel because those questions have become barriers.

How do we handle those barriers?

The simple answer is: By the grace of God and a few simple principles, we can answer their questions.

Why should we be interested in answering questions? The apostle Peter told us, "Sanctify Christ as Lord in your hearts, always being ready to make a defense to everyone who asks you to give an account for the hope that is in you, yet with gentleness and reverence" (1 Peter 3:15). Jude added, "I felt the necessity to write to you appealing that you contend earnestly for the faith which was once for all handed down to the saints" (v. 3).

The early Christians were always ready to give an account for the hope that was in them.[2] Answering questions, or apologetics, should occur whenever a question about the Christian faith arises in the natural conversation.

Now, keep in mind that apologetics is not the Gospel; it is a defense of the Gospel. Apologetics is a bridge for the Gospel to be shared. I might be able to answer somebody's questions; however, if I never get around to sharing the Good News with the unbeliever, that person is still lost! Apologetics is pre-evangelism. It provides the window of opportunity for the Gospel to be eventually shared. Notice also that 1 Peter 3:15 says that we should answer questions "with gentleness and reverence."

There is one main rule for the use of apologetics—"Gospel first, then apologetics."[3] That may sound like a contradiction. Didn't I just say apologetics occurs prior to evangelism? Well, yes, in sequence it does; but sometimes we choose to make the focus apologetics to the detriment of the Gospel. We stop short of sharing the Gospel, thinking the person needs evidence first. No; the person typically needs the Gospel first.

For example, a man in my evangelism class some years ago declared, "Every time I talk to someone about Jesus Christ, all that they want to talk about is the inerrancy of Scripture."

My response was simple. "Either God has you in a very unique environment where everyone around you wants to talk about the inerrancy of Scripture, or you are bringing the topic up yourself, and *you* really want to talk about the inerrancy of Scripture."

The man was upset that I could suggest such an option. A few weeks later he came back to me and confessed, "You know, you are right. I really do want to prove to everyone that the Bible is God's Word. I have been introducing the subject."

After coming to that realization, his conversations turned around. He found that not everyone wants to talk about the same subjects that he wanted to talk about.

If you keep the rule of "Gospel first, then apologetics" you will be spared from this tendency. If you start down the path toward sharing the Gospel, the questions that surface will be the questions that *they* want to ask and not the questions that *you* want to answer.

THINGS TO CONSIDER: USE EVIDENCE

When someone says about the Resurrection, "Prove it to me," I ask, "What will you accept as proof? If you are asking me to re-create the Resurrection, I can't do that. However, if you are asking me to present the evidence that the Resurrection is a historical fact, then we are talking."

First, remember that there is a difference between scientific proof and legal proof. We can only offer legal proof, not scientific proof. Scientific proof is proving something by repeating the event in the presence of the person questioning the fact. Legal proof proves things based upon the evidence and deals with things that are not repeatable.[4]

Scientific proof is valid with things that are repeatable. For example, maybe I say to you, "If I take beaker A and beaker B and mix them together, the mixture will explode."

"Prove it to me," you answer.

"All right; I can prove it to you. Here is beaker A, and here is beaker B. I mix them together . . ."

BOOM!

"See—they explode!"

I was able to prove that through the scientific method. In fact, I am able to repeat that as many times as you would like me to repeat it.

In contrast, legal proof deals with events that are not repeatable. History is a good example where legal proof is used. For example, how do we know that the Civil War took place? I can take you to the battlefields. I can show you pictures. I can show you some letters and artifacts, but I cannot re-create the Civil War. You will have to make a determination based upon the weight of the evidence. We deduce that the Civil War took place based upon the accumulated evidence, yet we are unable to repeat the Civil War.

There is an interesting point that must be made here. You may have all of the greatest evidence, and all of the best answers, and some people may still not believe. There are still a number of people out there that do not believe that the Holocaust took place! You can show them pictures; you can even present eyewitnesses. Yet for some reason they believe it is all a fabrication.

There are people who believe that the United States never landed on the moon. You can show them pictures and the black-and-white videotape of Neil Armstrong placing his feet onto the lunar landscape. You can show them moon rocks brought back. Yet they remain unbelievers. They are convinced that all the evidence has been assembled by staged photos and studio-produced TV footage (and rocks retrieved from the lunar surface by unmanned space probes) to make people think that the U.S. landed on the moon. In their minds, it never really happened.

This should show us that we may have the perfect reply to someone's questions or objections and the person still may choose not to believe. Even Jesus in His parable of the rich man and Lazarus noted that people would not believe even if someone rose from the dead (Luke 16:31). All God asks of you and me is to be faithful and leave the results in His hands. We are simply tools for Him to use.

THINGS TO CONSIDER: PEOPLE ARE DIFFERENT

Second, remember that people are different. How you answer one person might not be the same way that you answer someone else who asks the same question. There are hard-hearted people and soft-hearted people. Or as someone else has pointed out, "tough-minded" people and "tender-minded" people.[5] How I answer a soft-hearted person will not be the same way that I answer a hard-hearted person.

I remember walking into a private hospital room very early in my ministry to visit a man. As soon as I introduced myself, he exclaimed, "I have a question that no pastor, no minister, no chaplain has ever been able to answer!"

At that moment, I thought, "All right, is this man a hard-hearted person or a soft-hearted person?" His tone of voice and mannerisms led me to conclude that he was a little hard-hearted and was really out to win an argument more than anything else.

"All right, sir. Let me give it a try."

"Well, in Ephesians 14 it says that women are to keep silent and are not permitted to speak! They are supposed to ask their husbands at home and that it is shameful for women to speak in church! No one has been able to tell me why!"

This guy was coming across as a hard-hearted individual, so I needed to let the Holy Spirit work on him a bit. "Sir, there is a Bible right here. Let's look it up together. Unfortunately, Ephesians only has six chapters."

"Well, it must have been Galatians 14!" he said in a loud voice.

"Unfortunately, Galatians only has six chapters as well."

We examined a number of books (all the while I knew that the passage that he was looking for was 1 Corinthians 14:34–35). With

each book that we examined, his demeanor calmed down a little. He
started at a high pitch and it got lower as we went from book to book.

> Answer a soft-hearted person ... [differently] than ...
> someone who is antagonistic toward the Gospel.

Finally I said, "Sir, when I came in here you went right for my
jugular vein. I don't know you, and you don't know me. I am curious;
have you been hurt in the past by a minister or a chaplain?"

"No," he said. Then he went on to talk about all of the other
struggles going on in his life. After we had a wonderful conversation
about all different types of topics, including the Gospel, I asked, "Sir,
that passage you were looking for is in 1 Corinthians 14. Would you
like to take a look at it?"

"No," he said.

You see, his hard heart was a way to keep me away from his real
struggles. I would have never approached a soft-hearted person that
way; however, the way he came across indicated that a different approach was appropriate.

People are different. How you answer a soft-hearted person will be
a lot different than how you would answer someone who is antagonistic toward the Gospel. With someone who is more forceful and antagonistic toward the Gospel, I may be more aggressive and use what
some have called "offensive apologetics."[6] In other words, you are not
defending your position as much as you are asking him to defend his
position.

Suppose that a person asks, "How do you know that the Bible is
true?" Is this person hard-hearted or tenderhearted? If he is tenderhearted and asking a genuine question, wonderful! That is just the
type of person that I want to talk to. I will show him the evidence that
we have, talk about how we got our Bible, and answer questions.

However, if he is antagonistic and is looking for an argument, then I might turn the tables on the person and become more offensive by asking, "What evidence do you have that the Bible is not true?"

The way that I answer an individual will be determined by the way that the person comes across, his attitude. Jesus even handled questions differently. Consider the difference between the rich young ruler (Mark 10:17–31) and the woman at the well (John 4:7–30). With the ruler, Jesus took the offensive; with the woman He was tender and compassionate. Hopefully all of the people that you run into will be tenderhearted individuals looking for genuine answers to genuine questions. Unfortunately, that is not always the case. Be sure to handle the question wisely, because people are different.

GUIDELINES WHILE
ANSWERING QUESTIONS

Here are some general guidelines to follow while answering questions. Remember that each individual is different, and the way you answer one individual may not be the same way you answer someone else.

1. Pray. Most of all, pray for wisdom and sensitivity. As the apostle Paul wrote, "Conduct yourselves with wisdom toward outsiders, making the most of the opportunity. Let your speech always be with grace, seasoned, as it were, with salt, so that you will know how you should respond to each person" (Colossians 4:5–6). Pray that this might be true in your life.
2. Be sensitive. The person asking an honest question deserves an honest and sensitive answer. Watch out for pride and a condescending attitude in your approach. Make sure that you take enough time to define your terms and explain your answer fully.
3. Let the Holy Spirit work. Use Scripture whenever you can. Let the person wrestle with the Scriptures and not you when possible. There have been many times where Scripture is clear on

an issue, and all that I can do is point out the passage and let the unbeliever wrestle with God and not me. Gently point out that their argument is with God and not you. The Holy Spirit can do His work to convict of "sin and righteousness and judgment" (John 16:8).

4. Make Christ the center. The person that you want to hold out to a lost world is Jesus Christ, not you. Keep in mind that apologetics is a bridge to the Gospel. I might be able to answer all of an individual's questions; however, if I never get around to sharing the Gospel, then that person is still lost! Focus on God's grace and Christ's work.

With the man from India who had married an American girl, I never got around to the Gospel. He raised the question about God first, even though I was headed toward sharing the Gospel. And after talking with him for a while, I came to the conclusion that he wasn't ready to hear the Gospel. He was still wrestling with some pretty fundamental questions about the existence and nature of God.

TWO RULES FOR HANDLING QUESTIONS

As you respond to legitimate questions that are blocking an individual from hearing the Gospel, remember two rules. *First, start with a positive.* Affirm the person. Affirm the question. You might just say, "I'm really glad that you asked that question." Or, "I'm really glad that you made that statement. I appreciate your honesty. It does appear to be that way, doesn't it?" You might ask him how he feels about the question that he just raised.

You can say something nice about the question. Just saying, "Good question!" helps to build a rapport with the individual. It also gives you some time to think about how you are planning to respond.

And it can give you another indicator of whether this person is hard-hearted or tenderhearted.

Second, turn the question into a different question (after starting with a positive). There are a number of different reasons to do this; however, the main reason is to make sure that you are answering the question that the person really wanted to ask. Indeed, often I think that I have heard a particular question and I go off on a tangent, not answering the real question at all.

This reminds me of a story about Billy, who came to his mom and asked, "Mom, where did I come from?" Billy's mom assumes that he is asking about the birds and the bees and sits Billy down for a long talk. Billy's eyes get bigger and bigger as his mom talks about pollen, bees, boys, and girls. Finally she says, "Well, that's where you came from." Billy is sitting there with his mouth wide open and exclaims, "Wow, Bobby said that he came from Ohio!"

Billy's mom had just answered a question that Billy wasn't asking. By paraphrasing a question you are able to gain more information and discern some of their motives.

> Accumulate information that may
> help you to really address their concern.

For example, someone might object, "I believe that the church is full of hypocrites." Start with a positive. "Thanks! I appreciate your honesty. Let me ask you a question. What do you mean by hypocrite? Would you say that all Christians are hypocrites?"

"Well, not all Christians are hypocrites."

"How have you seen this in your life? Can you give me an example when somebody has been hypocritical?"

Now we are getting somewhere. You are beginning to accumulate information that may help you to really address their concern.

Someone else may state, "I have my own religion."

"Wow, that's super. Tell me about your religion."

Pause and let the person answer your question. Sometimes it is more effective to say nothing than something. The pause might give the person an opportunity to think about what has been said, or create some uneasiness in the person as he recognizes that he does not have an adequate answer.

I will then try to clarify some of the important doctrines of his religion. I might say, "Every religion has something out there [pointing out there somewhere]. Some call it God; some call it a force. Some are striving to get to heaven; some are trying to become one with a rock. What is 'out there' in your religion? What do you call that in your religion?"

Maybe he answers, "God."

"Terrific! Now tell me, what are you striving for? What do you call that?"

"Heaven."

"All right, now help me out. All religions have us down here [pointing around], don't they? We are all striving to make it to that place or thing 'out there.' There is a gap between 'out there' and 'right here,' correct?"

"Right."

"How do you bridge that gap?"

What I am doing with a person is letting him tell me what he thinks. Ultimately I am asking, "How does salvation take place in your religion?" In his religion, how does one become one with the force or arrive in the blissful state he describes?

It is easy to point out from any religion he describes that all religions have something "out there," and we have not arrived. We are striving through some type of work or merit to make it to the promised land.

Christianity is not a religion; it is a relationship. It is the only "religion" where we are not striving to make it, but God has come down to meet us. We don't have to do anything. Christ died for our sins, which was keeping us from Him, and arose from the dead. He died in our place.

Someone else objects, "Come on! Isn't the Bible full of errors and contradictions?"

Start with a positive. "Thanks for raising your concern."

Turn the question into a different question. "Which ones do you mean? Can you give me an example of the ones you are thinking about?"

Maybe you get into a lengthy discussion over a Bible passage and someone states emphatically, "Well, that's your interpretation!"

"What do you mean by interpretation?"

"Well, my interpretation is just as good as your interpretation."

"You know, the word *interpretation* means an explanation of the meaning. That means that the meaning the author intended is inherent within the text. The author intended to communicate something. If the author did not intend to communicate something, then there would not be any communication going on anywhere. All of that to say, you might be right and I might be wrong. Or I might be right and you might be wrong. Or we both might be wrong. However, we can't both be right!

"So, let's both go back and examine the text to see what the author intended to communicate."

Start with a positive and turn the question into a different question.

ANSWERING WITH GRACE

When I go to speak on evangelism, usually the fear that surfaces is, "Maybe they are going to ask me a question that I do not know." Let me encourage you by saying, They probably *will* ask you a question that you do not know! However, you can be honest and handle the question with grace and dignity.

It does not pay to get into an argument. Nobody ever wins an argument. The best-case scenario is a nice, quiet, intelligent discussion on the Bible and Jesus Christ.

You can answer questions with grace. Remember, "Gospel first, then apologetics." Start with a positive and turn the question into a new, clarifying question. Apologetics is a bridge to the Gospel. Answer questions with gentleness and reverence. May God richly use you in the process.

FIFTEEN:
HELPING
THEM GROW

EVANGELISM PRINCIPLE 7: *Disciple, nurture, and assimilate new believers into the church.*

A GOOD BUDDY and I decided to go to the Hare Krishna temple in Dallas to see what it was all about. We went in and sat down on the hardwood floor. At one end of the room was a plastic, lifelike statue of someone I did not recognize. There were pictures around the room that depicted a small, green, spiritlike being that I later found out were of Krishna, their deity. A man in a white robe with his head shaved came out and joined us on the floor.

After a few exchanges of pleasantries, my buddy asked, "What do you do all day?" He said the first thing followers do when they get up is chant. They are supposed to chant so many times. "Do you do that every morning?" my buddy asked.

"Not every morning."

"What else do you do?"

They have a regular routine they must follow. It involved a number of steps with repetitions at every turn. "Do you do all that every day?" my friend persisted.

"Not every day," said the man.

Here is where my buddy went into action. "You said that you were supposed to chant every morning so many times, and you don't do that. You then said that you were supposed to follow all of these routines every day and you don't do that. Everywhere that you have set up a standard for yourself, you fall short! How do you live with that?"

The man grew pale. He lowered his head and said quietly, "I grew up a Baptist."

What? He grew up going to a Baptist church! How in the world did this happen? Where was the breakdown in the system?

Now this man was probably not a believer. However, he had probably been sitting in the pews of a Bible-believing, Bible-teaching church for years, and apparently no one bothered to ask him about his relationship with Christ! And that's the point! *Nobody knew.*

There are lots of people sitting in our pews of whom we have no idea where they are in their relationship with Christ. And if someone says he or she is a believer, we may *assume* that the person has been followed up. Don't assume anything. We need to know.

One of the tragedies in the church today is that we are not doing a very good job in follow-up and discipleship. We talk a good talk, but unfortunately we do not walk a very good walk. With this young man, he probably heard the Gospel yet never trusted Jesus Christ personally for his salvation. He knew all the facts but had never appropriated those facts for himself. The breakdown in the system was that nobody had bothered to find out where this young man was in his relationship with Christ. He was a part of the church, but nobody bothered to know.

FOLLOW-UP VERSUS DISCIPLESHIP

I am going to make a distinction in this chapter between follow-up and discipleship. Follow-up usually happens with a *new believer* after he trusts Christ. Discipleship happens over a period of time with any believer. Follow-up starts the discipleship process. Since we are talking in this book specifically about evangelism, I will focus on using the term follow-up and refer to discipleship when I speak about "long-term follow-up." Obviously, the two overlap.

I have an important principle concerning follow-up. *Everybody should be following up somebody.* If everybody was following up somebody, then we would probably not have many cases like this young man. At least we would know. We all state that follow-up and discipleship are important; however, most of us are not involved. Personal follow-up greatly increases the spiritual development in a new believer's life.

When I travel, someone will inevitably ask, "Where are all the older men, or where are all the older women who are supposed to be discipling me?" The answer is, "You are that person!" You are the older man or the older woman to someone else! Somebody else is looking for you! At the same time, we cannot use our discipling as an excuse for not being involved in evangelism.

Notice that follow-up is part of the disciple-making process, yet it represents the final principle of evangelism. How does that work? The one who shares the Gospel and does the work of an evangelist still has a responsibility to the disciple-making process. It is not just an add-on —it is crucial for the evangelist to ground the new believer in his or her faith. Without follow-up, the evangelist is neglecting his responsibilities to a new believer. That is why follow-up is included as a principle of evangelism—to remind us that there is a disciple-making process involved.

In fact, *follow-up is the process of establishing a believer in the faith.* Notice two things about this definition. First, follow-up is a process and not just an event. We never arrive in follow-up. Secondly, the person being followed up may or may not be a new believer. There are a lot of people sitting in our pews who have never effectively been followed up.

There are three different kinds of follow-up: 1) immediate follow-up, 2) weekly follow-up, and 3) long-term follow-up.

By definition, immediate follow-up takes place immediately following a person expressing his trust in Jesus Christ. It happens in a period of minutes or hours. The primary focus is assurance. In contrast, weekly follow-up takes place over a period of weeks and accomplishes four goals, which we will explore later. Long-term follow-up takes place over a period of months and years. Let's look at each one briefly.

IMMEDIATE FOLLOW-UP

The primary goal with immediate follow-up is assurance. "Assurance is the realization that one possesses eternal life" and includes "the realization of the truth of eternal security or perseverance. A secure salvation is a true fact whether one realizes it or not. Thus a believer has security whether or not he has assurance."[1] If someone does not believe in the security of the believer, then he will most likely not have assurance. These two doctrines work closely together. When I talk about "assurance" I am linking these two doctrines. "The concept of eternal security emphasizes God's activity in guaranteeing the eternal possession of the gift of eternal life."[2]

There are a number of verses that you might want to turn to as you talk about assurance.[3] My favorite is John 5:24, where Jesus declares, "Truly, truly, I say to you, he who hears My word, and believes Him who sent Me, has eternal life, and does not come into judgment, but has passed out of death into life."

When I talk to an individual about this passage, I use a direct-question, logical-answer technique. I will say to the person, "It says that it is written to 'he who *hears* My word.' Have you heard His word?"

"Yes."

"'And *believes* in Him who sent Me.' Did you believe what God said and trust Christ as your Savior?"

"Yes."

"'*Has* eternal life.' Does that mean that you have eternal life now or later?"

"Now."

I would then continue in like fashion through the rest of the verse.

This technique of direct questions linked with logical answers is invaluable to help the new believer understand that he or she has eternal life. Assurance is not based upon feeling but upon the Word of God. Nothing can snatch a believer out of the Father's hand (John 10:29).

WEEKLY FOLLOW-UP

After the initial meeting, I will explore the option of getting together with him on a weekly basis for the next seven or eight weeks. There are really four goals that we should have in weekly follow-up. Get the new believer moving down these paths in the next eight weeks, and you can consider your time well spent.

The first goal for weekly follow-up is to help the new believer with assurance. Even though you have already talked about the concept in immediate follow-up, you will want to drill that concept into his head over the next eight weeks. Thus every week I will look at a new verse. I will also start having him memorize a verse a week to further solidify the principle. Some good verses to include are John 5:24; 10:27–30; Romans 8:38–39; and 1 John 5:11–13.

The second goal is to help the new believer develop a consistent personal devotional life. Now the problem with this particular goal is that it assumes that you are having a consistent personal devotional life! Once again, this is not a topic that you will talk about only once, but you will talk about his or her devotional life every week that you get together. There are a couple of important topics to cover under this umbrella.

The first topic is *prayer.* Not only do you want to talk to the new believer about the importance of prayer, but you should give him some insights into your own prayer life. For example, I manage my prayer life on 4 by 6-inch cards. Every category has a prayer "deck" and every prayer request has a 4 by 6-inch card. It is easy for me to write the requests on the card and then pray for them when they appear in the appropriate deck. The point is to help the new believer develop a way that feels comfortable in prayer. Share your approaches—and, in honesty, your struggles—in having a regular life of prayer with God.

The second topic is *Bible study.*[4] Talk about the difference between Bible study and Bible reading. Share with the new believer how you manage a regular time in God's Word.

> Consider inviting the new believer into
> your devotional time to observe what you do.

The third topic that you will want to talk about in developing a consistent personal devotional life is *personal worship.* We all seem to acknowledge that the essence of corporate worship is personal worship; however, we rarely explore the topic of personal worship.

Personal worship from my perspective needs to have a lot of variety. The more variety that takes place in my personal worship time the better. Sometimes I sing. Sometimes I do more Bible reading than Bible study. Sometimes I spend the entire time in prayer. Maybe I will maintain a journal for a season, maybe not. Each week is something different.

You may even want to consider inviting the new believer into your devotional time to observe what you do. Now I know that this is a sensitive issue for a lot of people; however, I can think of no better model. When I was doing an internship in California, the gentleman with whom I was doing the internship invited me into his devotional time for the entire three months. As I look back, I wish that I had been more attentive and had taken better notes. I had the opportunity to watch as he wrestled with Scripture and came to grips with some of the more difficult passages. What a gift he gave me! You have the opportunity to pass on that same gift to someone else.

Am I only going to talk about a personal devotional life once and then forget it? Of course not! Since this is a goal that I want to accomplish over a period of weeks, I will introduce the topic the first week and then come back to it every week that we are together.

The third goal for weekly follow-up is to help the new believer to understand some of the basics of the Christian life. What are some of the topics that you might want to explore? It depends upon the new believer. Most beginning follow-up books talk about assurance, prayer, Bible study, the Holy Spirit, and the importance of regular fellowship with a local body of believers. Other possible topics include baptism, confession, temptation, obedience, giving, evangelism, the ministry of the Holy Spirit, and memorizing Scripture.

If the individual is coming to you with some questions or problems in a specific area, you are certainly going to spend more time addressing those issues. For example, a young man might be wrestling with pornography. In that case, spending time talking about temptation and confession would be appropriate. Maybe a young couple has some questions regarding roles in marriage. Tailor the time for them and their growth in Christ. Each individual will be different.

If the person is just beginning with few presenting problems in his or her life, then you may want to consider using some of the resources that are available on the market. There are a number of good tools available that may just fit the need of the individual.[5]

Fourth, help the new believer become integrated into the life of a local church. This does not mean just taking the new believer to church; it means helping him become *integrated* into the life of the local church. It means helping the person get to the place where he feels a part of what is going on. Hopefully he will get to the place where he feels ministered to and also feels that he is able to contribute to the life of the body. His contribution may be minimal at first, but help him feel a part of the congregation. Introduce him to some people. Get him involved in a Sunday school class or a small group.

Is this going to happen in one week? Once again, of course not.

This goal will only be accomplished if I begin to work on it from week one. I certainly do not want to wait until week seven or eight to get started, because by then it will be too late.

The goals of weekly follow-up are four: to help the new believer to 1) have assurance, 2) develop a consistent personal devotional life, 3) understand some of the basics of the Christian life, and 4) become integrated into the life of a local church. If you can move a new believer down the road toward accomplishing these goals in seven or eight weeks, then you have made great strides in helping that new believer become a disciple of Christ.

A word of caution. Although immediate follow-up takes place in a matter of minutes and can be accomplished by the person who shared the Gospel, weekly and long-term follow-up require extended times together; therefore, they should occur only with someone of the same sex. Women should follow up women, and men should follow up men. If you have the opportunity to lead someone of the opposite sex to the Lord, then find someone appropriate in your church or organization to do the extended follow-up on that individual.

LONG-TERM FOLLOW-UP

After weekly follow-up there is another challenge for the believer that I believe we often overlook: long-term follow-up. This long-term follow-up takes place over the period of months and years. Follow-up becomes discipleship. Someone once said, "A student learns what his teacher knows. A disciple becomes what his master is."

A disciple means "a learner" or "a pupil, one who comes to be taught." A disciple can be a learner or a pupil of anything. Our goal is more specific. We are to make disciples of Jesus Christ. Luke 6:40 reads, "A pupil is not above his teacher; but everyone, after he has been fully trained, will be like his teacher."

J. Dwight Pentecost has identified three different types of disciples.[6] He talks about what he calls "curious disciples," those represented in John 6:60–66. These are people who are willing to study, but it is more of an intellectual pursuit. There is no life change, but following Christ is just entertainment to them, or a stimulant in their life. Then there are what Pentecost calls the "convinced disciple" (see John 6:67–69). These disciples are believers; however, there is no commitment. Lastly there are those who are "committed disciples" (see Luke 14:26–27, 33). These have made a commitment to follow Christ. You cannot be committed to Jesus Christ and not show it. This is the person who is focused, disciplined, and willing to sacrifice all for the cause of Jesus Christ.

> We are to . . . make committed disciples
> of Jesus Christ and not just inspiration junkies.

Pentecost wrote, "A true disciple is one who has a love for the person of Christ, confidence in the word of Christ, and is completely committed to Christ in service and obedience."[7] In fact, Christ lists a number of these characteristics as He identifies the committed disciple.[8]

It seems to me that we are to be in the business of helping to make committed disciples of Jesus Christ and not just inspiration junkies. If I am going to spend a significant amount of time with an individual, then I want to help him on that path toward total commitment.

A few disclaimers are in order here. First, none of us has arrived at Christlikeness. I am just one poor traveler helping another poor traveler along the path. I can teach, preach, coach, and counsel. However, the Holy Spirit working in that believer's life is the only One who is able to bring about lasting change. Second, you can be fooled. Paul had his Demas (2 Timothy 4:10) who, "having loved this present world," left Paul. It may appear that a certain person is ready to go for the Lord. However, something may come up in his or her life and cause the person to drift away from following Christ and to follow his or her own desires and ambitions instead.

You are just a tool that God is able to use. Be faithful to what He has called you to do.

Discipleship is a topic for another book. But when I get together with an individual for an extended time I am beginning to look for and develop some specific characteristics of a committed disciple.[9] Sometimes I will spend our entire year stimulating a supreme love for Jesus Christ, which is the first characteristic that I want to encourage. Other times I will spend our time going back to reinforce some of the principles that were introduced during the weekly follow-up. Maybe a book study is appropriate.

The point is to craft the time around where that disciple is currently wrestling. I am going to have to use discernment and skill to devise a curriculum that will help this disciple down the path toward greater maturity in Christ.

Follow-up of a new believer is crucial for his future growth and development. Follow-up can happen immediately, weekly, and over a long-term period. The goal is to help establish him in the faith. May God use you to help fulfill the Great Commission and make committed disciples of Jesus Christ.

A FINAL WORD

SO WHAT ABOUT YOU? In the spiritual life the question is not what you know, but what you are doing with what you know. The blessing is not in the knowing, but the blessing is in the doing (see John 13:17).

You are now responsible for the concepts presented in these pages. The issue is now between you and God.

Let me encourage you to take some risks for God. The adventure starts with your taking the first steps, not someone else taking the first steps. You have a choice to either ignore the teaching or begin to do something with it. As you begin to take some risks for God, you are in for the wildest and most fulfilling adventure ride of your life.

People are people no matter where they live in the world. People still wrestle with the root problem of sin no matter where they live. The strategies to reach people with the Gospel remain the same. The strategies presented in this book work. Just love people! Proclamational strategies, literature, relational strategies, acts of service, personal conversations, etc., are being used all over the world to reach people with the good news of Jesus Christ. The issue is not whether you have the equipment to get involved; the issue is whether you are willing to get involved.

May you be so yielded to the Spirit that you begin to see people the way that God sees people and love people the way that God loves people. So, get going! Just love people!

NOTES

Chapter 1: Fly the Airplane!

1. I was first introduced to this concept through the teaching ministry of Ray Ortlund. He delivered a series for the W. H. Griffith Thomas Memorial Lectures at Dallas Theological Seminary, November 4–7, 1980. They were later published in a four-article series entitled "Priorities for the Local Church," *Bibliotheca Sacra* 138, no. 549–52 (1981). They have been further adapted here.

2. Romans 13:8; cf. 1 Peter 1:22; 1 John 4:7.

3. Romans 12:16; 14:19; 15:14.

4. 1 Corinthians 12:25; Galatians 5:13; 6:2; Ephesians 4:32; 5:21, respectively.

Chapter 2. You Make the Call!

1. For a good discussion about the use of the word *evangelism,* see R. Larry Moyer, *Free and Clear* (Grand Rapids, Kregel, 1997), 161–65.

2. Lewis Sperry Chafer, *Systematic Theology,* vol. 7 (Dallas: Dallas Seminary, 1948), 143.

Chapter 3: How Does This All Fit Together?

1. Examples of authors who write from the relational strategy perspective include Joseph C. Aldrich, *Lifestyle Evangelism* (Portland: Multnomah, 1981) and Jim Petersen, *Living Proof* (Colorado Springs: NavPress, 1989). An example of an author from the aggressive strategy might be Mark McCloskey, *Tell It Often—Tell It Well* (San Bernardino, Calif.: Here's Life, 1986).

2. Michael Green, *Evangelism in the Early Church* (Grand Rapids: Eerdmans, 1970), 194.

3. The idea for this chart comes partly from James Engel's "The Spiritual-Decision Process," a classic scale found in James F. Engel and Wilbert Norton, *What's Gone Wrong with the Harvest?* (Grand Rapids: Zondervan, 1975), 45.

Chapter 4: How Open Are You?

1. The idea for the broad outline that has become the foundation for this chapter came from Michael Green, *Evangelism in the Early Church* (Grand Rapids: Eerdmans, 1970), 194–235.

2. See Acts 13:5, 14; 14:1; 17:1–2, 10, 16–17; 18:1, 4, 19; 19:8.

3. Frederic R. Howe, *Challenge and Response* (Grand Rapids: Zondervan, 1982), 20.

Chapter 5: Why Go Across the Street?

1. W. E. Vine, *Vine's Expository Dictionary of Old and New Testament Words* (Old Tappan, N.J.: Revell, 1981), 335.

2. It has been suggested that the participle "go" really carries with it the force of the imperative. See J. Ronald Blue, "Go Missions," *Bibliotheca Sacra* 141 (October–December, 1984): 341–53.

3. From a private conversation with Jeffery L. Townsend, missionary and teacher, 4 June 2002.

4. It's true that Paul said that he still rejoiced whenever the Gospel was preached, even from wrong motives: "What then? Only that in every way, whether in pretense or in truth, Christ is proclaimed; and in this I rejoice, yes, and I will rejoice" (Philippians 1:18). However, our responsibility is to make sure that our motives are correct.

Chapter 6: What Did You Say?

1. This is our word *euangelion* that we explored in chapter 2.

2. Charles C. Ryrie, *So Great Salvation* (Wheaton, Ill.: Victor, 1989), 23–24.

3. Ibid., 22.

4. Ibid., 37–39.

5. Ibid., 38.

6. The root meaning of the Hebrew word most frequently used for "sin," *chatah,* is "miss (a goal or way), go wrong, sin." See Francis Brown, S. R. Driver, and Charles A. Briggs, *A Hebrew and English Lexicon of the Old Testament* (Oxford: Clarendon, 1980), 306–7.

7. Charles C. Ryrie, *Basic Theology* (Wheaton, Ill.: Victor, 1986), 212.

8. Lewis Sperry Chafer, *Systematic Theology,* vol. 7 (Dallas: Dallas Seminary, 1948), 287.

9. R. Larry Moyer, *Free and Clear* (Grand Rapids: Kregel, 1997), 29.

10. Ryrie, *Basic Theology*, 218.

11. Ibid., 223.

12. Ibid., 224.

13. For a good discussion on the word *atonement* see Chafer, *Systematic Theology*, 25–27.

14. Douglas M. Cecil, "The Emphasis of the Resurrection in the Apostles' Preaching in the Book of Acts Compared to Current Evangelistic Emphases" (Th.M. thesis, Dallas Theological Seminary, 1984).

15. The word used in Genesis 15:6 for Abraham's faith is the Hebrew word *aaman*. The root is used in the word for a pillar and describes the pillars of the Temple (2 Kings 18:16). Temple pillars are something that can be relied upon. You can put weight on them and trust them to hold up the roof. In the Hiphil stem the word means to believe, as in Genesis 15:6 (see Brown, Driver, and Briggs, *A Hebrew and English Lexicon of the Old Testament*, 52–53). In Romans 4:3–5, Paul states that our faith is like Abraham's faith.

16. This analogy is adapted from an illustration in G. Michael Cocoris, *Evangelism: A Biblical Approach* (Chicago: Moody, 1984), 77.

Chapter 7: Springing from the Inside Out

1. Dwight Edwards' message entitled "Drink from Running Torrents!" at the "Think World" missions conference, Dallas Theological Seminary, 5 March 1996, was of great help in the main outline of this passage. The main outline and teaching of Edwards is used here by permission, and his message is the basis of a book to be published in the fall of 2003 by WaterBrook Press.

2. Chaim Richman, *The Holy Temple of Jerusalem* (Jerusalem: The Temple Institute & Carta, 1997), 63–69.

3. Ibid., 65.

4. Deuteronomy 16:13 says that the feast went for seven days. Leviticus 23:36 indicates that the feast had an eighth day, which was a "holy convocation." Leon Morris, *The Gospel According to John* (Grand Rapids: Eerdmans, 1971), 420–21, takes "the last day of the feast" (John 7:37) as being on the eighth day. However, Alfred Edersheim, *The Life and Times of Jesus the Messiah* (Grand Rapids: Eerdmans, 1971), 2:156–163 and J. Dwight Pentecost, *The Words and Works of Jesus Christ* (Grand Rapids: Zondervan, 1981), 279–82, understands the last day of the feast to be the seventh day. I agree with Edersheim and Pentecost and understand the eighth day to be separate from the seven-day feast.

5. According to Richman, *The Holy Temple of Jerusalem*, 64: "The one to the east was for the wine libations that were poured during the daily *tamid* sacrifice; the other was designated for this service, which took place exclusively on Sukkot."

6. After this pastor had said this to me, the phrase showed up in Gail MacDonald, *High Call, High Privilege* (Wheaton, Ill.: Tyndale, 1981), 18. I do not know where the phrase first originated.

7. Lewis Sperry Chafer, *True Evangelism* (Grand Rapids: Kregel, 1993), 81–95.

8. Ibid., 95.

Chapter 8: Being Faithful

1. The program and approach being described is called Evangelism Explosion. More information about E. E. can be found in D. James Kennedy, *Evangelism Explosion* (Wheaton, Ill.: Tyndale, 1970).

2. These broad categories of creation, conscience, Scripture, the Holy Spirit, Christians, and circumstances were suggested in Michael P. Green, "Evangelism" (Unpublished class notes, Dallas Theological Seminary, Spring 1991), 45. Used by permission.

3. Lindsay Terry, *The Amazing Story Behind "Amazing Grace"* (Garland, Texas: American Tract Society, 1996), 1.

4. Terry, *The Amazing Story,* 4.

5. F. Deauville Walker, *William Carey* (Chicago: Moody, 1980), 42, 232.

Chapter 9: Are You Passive or Active?

1. "History of the U. S. Postal Service: Pony Express," on the Internet at http://www.usps.com/history/his2.htm PONY. Accessed on 3 March 2003.

2. "City of St. Joseph: The Pony Express," on the Internet at http://www.ci.st-joseph.mo.us/pony.html. Accessed on 3 March 2003.

3. See chapter 3. Disciple making is the process that begins with being a witness prior to sharing the Gospel, which is prior to conversion.

4. Joseph C. Aldrich, *Gentle Persuasion* (Portland: Multnomah, 1988), 7–8.

5. Other examples of acts of service can be found in Joseph C. Aldrich, *Lifestyle Evangelism* (Portland: Multnomah, 1981), and Steve Sjogren, *Conspiracy of Kindness* (Ann Arbor, Mich.: Servant, 1993).

6. Jim Petersen, *Living Proof Video Series* (Colorado Springs: NavPress, 1990), Session 7.

7. Petersen, *Living Proof* (Colorado Springs: NavPress, 1989), 126.

Chapter 10: Becoming Real

1. Margery Williams, *The Velveteen Rabbit* (New York: Avon, 1975), 16–17.

2. This concept was first suggested to me by Michael P. Green, "Evangelism" (Unpublished class notes, Dallas Theological Seminary, Spring 1991), 48–49; later published as "The Purpose of Evangelism," James D. Berkley, ed., *Leadership Handbook of Practical Theology,* vol. 2 (Grand Rapids: Baker, 1994), 9–10. The concept has been slightly modified; however, the basic premise is the same.

3. Joe Aldrich, in his book *Life-Style Evangelism* (Portland, Ore.: Multnomah, 1981), page 221, talks about his pilgrimage question. I have always found it helpful in proceeding in that direction.

Chapter 11: Send in the Herd!

1. R. Larry Moyer, *Free and Clear* (Grand Rapids: Kregel, 1997), 176.

2. For more ideas on how to maximize the effectiveness of a small church, see Ron Klassen and John Koessler, *No Little Places* (Grand Rapids: Baker, 1996).

Chapter 12: Tell Your Story

1. The "ABCs" are expanded from the list in Ron Rand, *Won by One* (Venture, Calif.: Regal, 1988), 159-60.

Chapter 13: A Natural Extension of You and Your Ministry

1. C. H. Spurgeon, *The Soul Winner* (New Kensington, England: Whitaker, 1995), 231.

2. Lewis Sperry Chafer, *True Evangelism* (Grand Rapids: Kregel, 1993), 78.

3. Ibid., 71.

4. Ibid., 69.

5. To explore these concepts I would encourage you to reference Charles C. Ryrie, *Basic Theology* (Wheaton, Ill.: Victor, 1986).

6. Larry Moyer, *Free and Clear* (Grand Rapids: Kregel, 1997), 52–55 records the "Good News–Bad News" presentation. It is also available from EvanTell, P.O. Box 741417, Dallas, TX 75374-1417. Or you can call their toll-free number at 1-800-947-7359.

7. Chafer, *True Evangelism*, 72–73.

Chapter 14: Answering Questions

1. Frank Morison, *Who Moved the Stone?* (1930; reprint, Grand Rapids: Zondervan, 1987).

2. For example, see Paul in Acts 17:2–4, 19–34; 18:4, 19; 19:8–10, 26; 22:1–21; 26:1–29; 28:23–24; or Apollos in Acts 18:28.

3. This principle is articulated well in Dan Story, *Engaging the Closed Minded* (Grand Rapids: Kregel, 1999), 35, as "Gospel First, Apologetics Second." I cannot improve upon his simple explanation. Apologetics is pre-evangelism; it is not evangelism.

4. Paul E. Little, *Know Why You Believe* (Downers Grove, Ill.: InterVarsity, 1968), is a great little book that helps to think through these issues.

5. Story, *Engaging the Closed Minded*, 27.

6. Ibid., 27–33.

Chapter 15: Helping Them Grow

1. Charles C. Ryrie, *Basic Theology* (Wheaton, Ill.: Victor, 1986), 328.

2. Ibid.

3. Passages might include 1 John 5:11–13; John 5:24; Romans 8:38–39; and John 10:27–28.

4. A great book to study in this regard is Howard G. Hendricks and William D. Hendricks, *Living by the Book* (Chicago: Moody, 1991).

5. Among the books that you may want to consider is R. Larry Moyer, *Welcome to the Family* (Grand Rapids: Kregel, 1996), or his book entitled *Growing in the Family* (Grand Rapids: Kregel, 2000). Other organizations like the Navigators or Campus Crusade for Christ have great follow-up material. Gary W. Kuhne, *The Dynamics of Personal Follow-up* (Grand Rapids: Zondervan, 1976), is a great book for follow-up topic ideas.

6. J. Dwight Pentecost, *Design for Discipleship* (Grand Rapids: Zondervan, 1971), 14–21.

7. Ibid., 20.

8. I would highly recommend to you the book by Mark Bailey, *To Follow Him* (Sisters, Oreg.: Multnomah, 1997). This book lists seven marks of a committed disciple.

9. Ibid.

Since 1894, Moody Publishers has been dedicated to equip and motivate people to advance the cause of Christ by publishing evangelical Christian literature and other media for all ages, around the world. Because we are a ministry of the Moody Bible Institute of Chicago, a portion of the proceeds from the sale of this book go to train the next generation of Christian leaders.

If we may serve you in any way in your spiritual journey toward understanding Christ and the Christian life, please contact us at www.moodypublishers.com.

"All Scripture is God-breathed and is useful for teaching, rebuking, correcting and training in righteousness, so that the man of God may be thoroughly equipped for every good work."
—2 TIMOTHY 3:16, 17

MOODY
PUBLISHERS
THE NAME YOU CAN TRUST®

THE 7 PRINCIPLES OF AN EVANGELISTIC LIFE TEAM

ACQUIRING EDITOR:
Mark Tobey

COPY EDITOR:
Jim Vincent

BACK COVER COPY:
Julie Allyson-Ieron, Joy Media

COVER DESIGN:
Barb Fisher, LeVan Fisher Design

INTERIOR DESIGN:
Ragont Design

PRINTING AND BINDING:
Versa Press Incorporated

The typeface for the text of this book is
AGaramond